THE WEDDING DRESS

THE WEDDING DRESS

300 YEARS OF BRIDAL FASHIONS

Edwina Ehrman

V&A PUBLISHING

First published by V&A Publishing, 2011
Victoria and Albert Museum
South Kensington
London SW7 2RL
www.vandapublishing.com

This edition published 2014

Distributed in North America by Harry N. Abrams, Inc., New York

Hardback edition
ISBN 978 1 85177 813 3

Library of Congress Control Number 2011923017

10 9 8 7 6 5 4 3 2
2018 2017 2016 2015 2014

Paperback edition
ISBN 978 1 85177 783 9

Library of Congress Control Number 2013495520

10 9 8 7 6 5 4 3
2018 2017 2016 2015 2014

Designer: Nigel Soper
Copy-editor: Mark Kilfoyle
Index: Vicki Robinson

New photography by Richard Davis, V&A Photographic Studio

Front cover illustration: Jasper Conran, Autumn/Winter 2007.
Photograph by Tessa Traeger. Courtesy of Jasper Conran

Back cover illustration: *Qui a le driot* by Christian Lacroix Haute
Couture, Autumn/Winter 1992–3. Photograph by Guy Martineau.
V&A: T.241:1 to 16–1933. Given by Christian Lacroix

Frontispiece: Wedding dress, 1950s. Photograph by Lillian Bassman.
V&A: PH.12–1986. © Lillian Bassman

p.6: Wedding favour. Wax, cloth, paper and silk, British, 1889.
V&A: T.266A–1971. Given by Mrs V.I. Lewin

Printed in China

CONTENTS

'Mary from top to toe was immaculate in white and looked better than ever I had seen her. But I think in general all brides do – it does not, I believe, proceed from their being more than ordinary beautiful, but they are more than ordinary interesting. The eternal union of two hearts very strangely engages our own, and makes us strongly picture the future or remember the past.'

MARTHA LE MESURIER
to her Aunt, 15 September 1779 [1]

INTRODUCTION

This book describes the history of the white wedding dress in Britain from its antecedents in the eighteenth century to the present day. At its core is the Victoria and Albert Museum's superb collection of fashionable wedding dress. The collection comprises just over 200 wedding garments and accessories ranging in date from 1673 to 2007 (see pp.188–97). Apart from a small group of mid-nineteenth-century men's wedding garments, the majority of the pieces were worn by brides.

The Museum acquired its first example of wedding dress in 1900, when it purchased a coat and breeches made of white silk brocaded with silver-gilt threads. The suit was reputedly made for Sir Thomas Isham (1657–81) for his marriage in 1681. It was one of a group of garments associated with the Isham family which were acquired because they exemplified the cut, construction and fabrics of their period.[1] The first wedding dress entered the collection two years later. Its bodice is inscribed, 'Jean Smith married 20th April 1789' (pl.27). The dress, which is made from blue and white striped silk patterned with tiny white stars, zigzags and baskets of flowers, is now very fragile.[2] It too was purchased, but thereafter the majority of wedding garments collected by the Museum were gifts from the wearers or their descendants who wanted to find a good home for a treasured family possession where it would be appreciated, studied and preserved. Many of the twentieth-century dresses were given with original photographs that show how the outfits were worn. Often displaying accessories that no longer survive, the images further our insight into the social aspect of dress – its relationship to the body, to class and social aspiration, and how women present themselves as 'brides'. Wedding clothes, like other types of dress, reflect the societies that create and make ceremonial use of them. They can illustrate responses to technological change and shifts in the economy, and reflect changing attitudes towards the wedding ceremony and marriage. Dresses with a proven history are also valuable dated specimens which can be compared with other dated material to help establish when particular styles were introduced and how long they remained fashionable.

The majority of the wedding garments in the V&A collection were designed and made in Britain. The Museum's focus on collecting objects that exemplify good design and high standards of manufacture has ensured that many of the country's leading couturiers and designers are represented. With outstanding dresses by designers such as Norman Hartnell (pls 1–2), the book reflects this strength. Of the garments made overseas there is a small group of wedding clothes made and worn in the United States of America. Two pieces are described and illustrated in chapter three to show wedding styles common to Britain and North America which cannot be represented by British garments in the collection. The European wedding dresses are almost all French and a couture bridal dress generously donated by designer Christian Lacroix (b.1951) has been included in chapter six to provide a comparison with British couture bridal wear in the early 1990s (pl.133).

The book links wedding outfits in the Museum's collection to contemporary accounts of weddings found in diaries, letters, memoirs and newspapers to create a chronological survey of the white wedding dress. Its six chapters cover periods of varying length determined by a combination of changes in wedding fashions and major events, such as the marriage of Queen Victoria in 1840 and the two world wars in the twentieth century. They consider the impact of legal, social, cultural, economic and technological change on bridal fashions and explore how wedding garments were designed, made, marketed, sold and worn. For most of the period under discussion, wedding dress styles followed the fashions of their period and throughout the book wedding garments are described in the wider context of fashionable dress. Royal wedding garments are described in some detail as they were often translated into popular styles.[3] From chapter two, which covers 1790–1840, each chapter introduces new ways of communicating bridal fashions, from fashion illustrations and photographs in the nineteenth century to film, television and the internet in the twentieth and twenty-first centuries.

In the eighteenth century some wealthy women chose to wear white silk dresses for their weddings,

1 Margaret Whigham and Charles Sweeny, 1933. Darlings of the gossip columns, the glamorous couple brought traffic to a standstill when they married at London's Brompton Oratory. As Duchess of Argyll, Whigham would later be the subject of a notorious divorce case.
© Hulton-Deutsch Collection / CORBIS

2 Silk satin wedding dress
(front and back) by Norman Hartnell, London, 1933. Margaret Whigham commissioned the dress from the celebrated couturier for her marriage to Charles Sweeny on 21 February 1933.

V&A: T.836–1974. Given and worn by Margaret, Duchess of Argyll

but other colours and patterned silks were also popular for brides. At the highest levels of society silver, and white and silver, vied with white as the most prestigious and fashionable bridal colours until white became the colour of choice in the early nineteenth century. As the dominant religion in Britain and France (whose bridal fashions influenced those worn in Britain for most of the period the book covers), Christianity's association of white with innocence and purity was an important symbolic factor. Even today, in Britain's increasingly secular society, the white wedding dress has lingering connotations of virginity. White garments were associated with spiritual rites of passage long before they became conventional for bridal wear. Babies have been dressed in white robes for the sacrament of baptism when they are initiated into the Christian faith since the eighteenth century. The choice of white garments may be linked to the pre-Reformation use of the white chrisom-cloth, which was placed on the baby's head or wrapped around its body after baptism and symbolized its innocence.[4] Children who died within a month of baptism were buried in the chrisom-cloth, and white continued to be associated with the funerals of children and unmarried men and women into the early twentieth century. White was also worn for general mourning because of its absence of positive colour and association with purity.[5] Most of the brides and grooms referred to in the text whose faith is known were members of the Christian church, but some were of the Jewish faith and another was a Buddhist. Since the Second World War people from many different faiths and ethnic groups with their own wedding customs have made their homes in Britain, but British society as a whole has become less religious. In 2008 civil ceremonies accounted for 67% of all marriage ceremonies.[6]

White was also a status symbol in the centuries when laundry had to be done laboriously by hand, without the aid of gas or electricity to heat water, and hung out to dry. Dry cleaning had not been invented. It was difficult to keep white underclothes fresh and clean; delicate white outer garments took skill as well as time and effort to maintain. Wealthy women could afford to pay servants to care for their clothes, but for the less well-off white was not a prudent choice. Most women from more modest backgrounds chose coloured wedding dresses and the V&A has several nineteenth-century examples. In this book the double-page spreads between the chapters offer a counterpoint to white wedding attire by focusing on examples of coloured wedding dresses and the reasons for their selection. Other coloured dresses are described in the final chapter which touches on clothing chosen for civil partnership ceremonies and ceremonies at which couples reaffirmed their vows following civil marriages.

Most of the weddings described in the book took place in England but the brides and grooms came from across Britain. To reflect this geographical spread, the terms Britain and British have been used in the text but when the exact location of a wedding or the nationality of a person is known, it has been stated. The adjective 'British' has also been used to describe fashions made and worn in Britain. Britain has a long history of copying, assimilating and adapting the fashions of other countries, particularly France, making it difficult to define exactly what constitutes British fashion. Certain types of clothing and attitudes to dressing are thought to be particularly British. British women have traditionally valued practicality, style and individuality above precise adherence to the fashionable look promoted in fashion plates or on the catwalk. However this preference for comfortable, unaffected but well-made clothes was balanced by an acknowledgement of the importance of dressing up for formal occasions such as weddings. Some women used this opportunity to introduce an element of fantasy into their clothes and this British taste for dressing-up can be seen in the popularity of romantic wedding styles which draw on the cut, construction and decorative details of historical dress. Tailored menswear is also identified as being particularly British and until comparatively recently most British bridegrooms from the upper and middle classes wore suits with frock coats or morning coats for their weddings. Men in other countries have also worn these garments, but British men have been credited with a more nuanced approach to dressing that allows for self-expression within the strictures of conventional dress.[7] In the twenty-first century fashion is international, but people from different countries and regions continue to dress in subtly different ways.

Genealogical research has been an important tool for providing a context for garments in the V&A's collection. By using the census and other records, it has been possible to discover information about the occupations, circumstances and faiths of many wearers. Such details personalize the garments and bring their histories to life. They also give some idea of the social level of the wearer and help us understand dress as a commodity within a much larger network of trade and global development. Julia, Mary and Edith Montefiore donated their father's wedding waistcoat to the V&A in 1919, having carefully stitched a label to it detailing its provenance (pl.3). Sources revealed that John Montefiore (1820–95), a London merchant dealing in goods from the West Indies, was the son of John Castello Montefiore (1790–1854), a plantation owner and merchant in Barbados. Just seven when slavery

3 Figured silk waistcoat,
British, 1845, and detail of
the label stitched to it by the
wearer's daughters. John
Montefiore, whose wealth
derived from trade in the
West Indies, wore this
waistcoat for his marriage to
Julia Norman in London on
28 January 1845.

V&A: T.668–1919. Given by the Misses
Montefiore in memory of the late John
Montefiore, Esq.

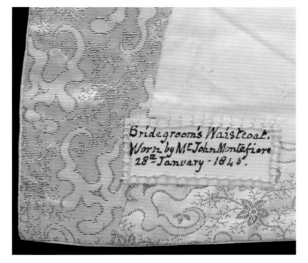

was abolished in the British West Indies in 1827, he and his father are still commemorated in Barbados by a public drinking fountain the son gave to the city of Bridgetown in 1864 in memory of his father, who had died from cholera ten years earlier. The link between a figured silk waistcoat, international trade and the profits of slavery is an important one to recall. Another wedding garment, worn by Sarah Boddicott for her marriage to her second cousin Samuel Tyssen in 1779 (see pl.26), is also linked to slavery through their families' business interests in the Caribbean. The Tyssen family owned sugar plantations in Antigua and Sarah Boddicott's grandfather was a sugar merchant and insurer in London.[8] The wealth of families involved in the slave trade came at a considerable moral cost as the slaves forcibly brought to the Caribbean to work on the sugar plantations laboured in particularly harsh and dangerous conditions.

Periodicals and national and regional newspapers targeting readers from a range of social and economic backgrounds offer a wealth of historical detail. Articles and advertisements provide information on wedding fashions and their makers, suppliers and cost, descriptions of actual weddings and satirical commentary, often drawing attention to the high cost of weddings. Several descriptions were found of weddings represented by garments in the V&A collection. They include the wedding of the Reverend Andrew Nugée and Elizabeth Wroughton Richards, which took place at Farlington Church in Hampshire in 1854 and was reported by the *Hampshire Telegraph*. The article did not mention the bride's dress but described twelve 'tastefully dressed' schoolgirls who carried specially made baskets containing flowers that they scattered in the path of the bridal couple as they left the church.[9] In 2008 descendants of the couple donated a fascinating group of objects associated with the wedding to the Museum. They include shoes, a beautiful and unusual wreath made from green and white feathers skilfully manipulated to resemble orange-blossom, and wedding favours of orange-blossom, lilies of the valley and hawthorn blossom made from cloth and garnished with oak leaves of silvered paper (pls 4–5). The Nugée family's careful preservation of these fragile mementos for over a hundred and fifty years is evi-

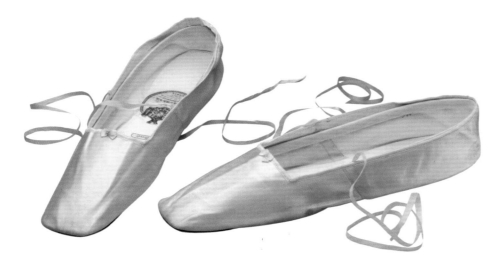

4 Silk satin slippers made by Chapelle, Paris, c.1854. Newspaper descriptions of weddings are a rich source of information. When the Reverend Andrew Nugée wed Elizabeth Wroughton Richards, who wore these slippers, the event was reported in the *Hampshire Telegraph*.

V&A: T.4:1, 2–2008.
Given by Edward Nugée QC

5 Wedding wreath and favours, dyed feathers, cotton, silk and paper, British, 1854. The accessories conjure up the romantic prettiness of many Victorian weddings.

V&A: T.6 to 8–2008.
Given by Edward Nugée QC

dence of their value to the family. Together the objects and news report conjure up the romantic prettiness typical of many Victorian weddings.

Until the twentieth century most wedding dresses were worn again after the wedding day for 'Sunday best' or for special occasions. They were often adapted and altered to prolong their life. In spite of this many women chose to preserve their dresses because of the significance of their marriage ceremony for them. Some garments attain the status of family heirlooms and are passed down through several generations. Their provenance often becomes confused, as stories about the dress evolve over time, but their tangible link to the family's past guarantees their survival. Children can be particularly moved by their parents' wedding clothes. When Miss Helen Bright offered the V&A her mother's wedding dress, veil and shoes in May 1945 (pls 6–9), she explained that she would like to bequeath them on her death because 'at present I do not wish to part with them'. She assured the Museum of their excellent condition and added that the dress 'is greatly admired by all who see it'. Her words suggest the pleasure and comfort she took in her mother's clothes and the enjoyment she derived from sharing them with others, making a museum an appropriate home for them.

6 Silk satin wedding dress trimmed with Honiton lace, and a Honiton lace veil (detail overleaf), British, 1864–5. Eliza Penelope Clay wore the dress when she married Joseph Bright, a landowner from Derbyshire, at St James's Church, Piccadilly, London, on 16 February 1865.

V&A: T.43&A–1947.
Given by Miss H.G. Bright

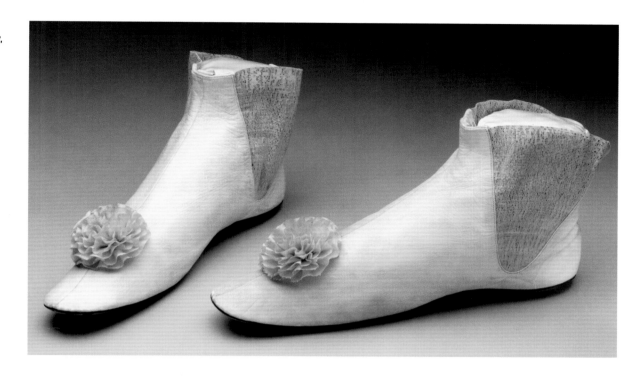

7 Honiton lace veil (detail) worn by Eliza Penelope Clay, British, 1864–5.
V&A: T.43A–1947.
Given by Miss H.G. Bright

8 Silk and leather ankle boots, French or British, c.1865. Like many women, Helen Bright took immense pleasure in her mother's wedding ensemble, which she kept until her death.
V&A: T.43B&C–1947.
Given by Miss H.G. Bright

9 Letter from Miss Helen Bright, 10 May 1945.
V&A: T.43–1947

> May 10 – 1945.
>
> Dear Sir
>
> I am in possession of a beautiful cream satin dress, worn by my Mother at her wedding to my Father at St James's, Piccadilly, in Feb.y 1865, & a veil of lace, which I am told is Honiton. The dress has a deep flounce of similar lace upon the skirt.
>
> All is in perfect preservation, & is greatly admired by all who see it. At present I do not wish to part with them: but would offer them to the Victoria & Albert Museum, & make arrangements about them with my executors. Friends from London have urged

Such feelings have not disappeared. In 2005, the writer Justine Picardie expressed similar emotions about her mother's wedding dress. When she touched and tried on the expensive black French cocktail dress and jacket her mother had mysteriously chosen, she felt protective towards her. She reflected on her youthful slenderness, but she was also reminded, as she observed the dress's wrinkled lining, of how women age and by implication of her own mortality. Described by Picardie as a 'precious bequest', the dress provoked questions her mother could not answer satisfactorily, frustrating her daughter's wish to understand her and her mother's joint past through the material of the dress. Her realization that she had later lost the outfit caused the author pain. She felt that the past was 'eluding' her, 'as if I [had] lost a piece of my heart'.[10]

Since the introduction of commercial photography in the mid-nineteenth century, wedding photographs have also been treasured and preserved, often in special albums or framed for display. They provide a rich resource of information about weddings, their attire and social attitudes. Dress and photographs offer different ways of reaching back into the past. The experience of handling fabric – its texture, smell and stains; the dust on the hem; a smudge of lipstick – prompts a very subjective, physical response. Photographs on the other hand offer a record of what took place and their sequence or grouping in an album conveys a narrative. How such photographs are treated is revealing. If an album is prepared by a professional photographer, the photographic series will usually follow certain conventions. The bridal couple or a family member is likely to pro-

10 African wedding in Costa do Sol, Maputo, Mozambique, 2004. The spread of Christianity has encouraged many African brides to wear white wedding dresses.

Photograph by Corina Gertz.
© Corina Gertz

11 Japanese wedding at Kaiyukan Aquarium, Maki and Nobuyuki Tamanishi, Osaka, 29 July 2006. The white wedding dress has become a global phenomenon. Japanese brides often hire a white dress as one of several outfits to wear during the course of their marriage celebrations.

© 2006 AFP / Getty Images

duce something more idiosyncratic, making more personal juxtapositions and annotating the images. Whatever form they take, photographs also become a material part of a family's history. Turning the pages of a wedding album or handling a specially framed photograph that marks the occasion can create a powerful tangible link between past and present.

Weddings and wedding dresses remain a perennial cultural interest. Every year newspapers and magazines feature articles about weddings. They frequently cite the latest statistics about marriage in modern Britain. According to the Office for National Statistics the provisional number of marriages registered in England and Wales in 2008 was 232,990. (When the full figure is known this is expected to rise by up to 1%.) This is the lowest marriage rate since it was first calculated in 1862. However the divorce rate is at its lowest rate since 1979, suggesting that those who choose to marry are more committed to making it work.[11] For women who decide to marry in church rather than in a registry office, wearing white symbol-

12 British wedding in Wiltshire, 19 July 2008. Edward and Nina Tryon married at the Church of St Mary and St Nicholas, Wilton. Philip Treacy designed the bride's headdress and Vivienne Westwood her dress.

Photograph by Kevin Davies.
© Kevin Davies

izes their commitment to marriage but also fulfils an emotional need, making them feel like a bride embarking on a new phase of their life. Women who have worn white for their weddings talk about its romantic, fairy-tale appeal and talismanic qualities, but above all of how it miraculously transformed them into a bride. In the nineteenth and early twentieth centuries, the white wedding dress was the preserve of well-to-do women in Europe and the USA, but today

it is worn by brides of many faiths across the world to celebrate their marriages (pls 10–15). The commercialization of weddings, particularly in the Middle East and East Asia, and the globalization of fashion has fuelled this trend. In Christian communities the religious associations of the white wedding dress remain important, but for women of other faiths the white wedding dress today is a symbol of wealth, status, modernity and romantic love.

13 American wedding in Setauket, New York, 26 August 2007. Katie Bella Turner wore a Vera Wang dress from the designer's Spring 2007 bridal collection for her marriage to Andrew Hayward.

Photograph courtesy of the bride

14 Canadian wedding in Digby, Nova Scotia, 21 August 2010. Canadian law permits same-sex couples to marry. When Linday Laton and Karen McNolty wed, both women chose to wear traditional white gowns.

Photograph by Jason Wolsky

15 British wedding in New Forest, Hampshire, 27 March 2010. Gity Monsef wore a dress designed by her friend Dennis Nothdruft for her marriage to Gary Webb, who wore a Savile Row suit.

Photograph by Irina Voiteleva

SILVER AND WHITE

1700–90

In the eighteenth century the social and economic status of the bride and groom, where and when the wedding service took place and the importance of their guests were determining factors in what the bride wore. From 1700–90, there was no one consistently popular colour for wedding dresses but the evidence suggests that there were class preferences. Letters and diaries show that aristocratic and very wealthy brides often chose silver, white and silver, and white bridal clothes (pl.16). These colours were not exclusive to weddings and were worn on other formal occasions. White was also popular for summer clothes. There are fewer published contemporary documents which describe how brides from the gentry and middling classes dressed but garments which survive in museums suggest that they wore a range of colours. New clothes were customary for those who could afford them but no eighteenth-century bride would have expected to wear her wedding clothes for a single occasion and accordingly most extant dresses have been modified to reflect changes in fashion and the wearer's figure. Brides with limited funds simply wore their best dress.

For the propertied classes getting married involved a formal betrothal and the negotiation of a legal contract which established the financial arrangements on which the marriage would be conducted (pl.17). The acceptance of a proposal of marriage was a family decision based on the financial and social standing of the prospective bridegroom as much as on his character. Most parents hoped for mutual affection between the couple but a prudent choice was more important than passion.[1] The wedding took place as soon as possible after the marriage contract had been signed. Some women were married hours later, most within a month. Marriage was a momentous step and many women found the prospect of leaving home to create a new life with their husband daunting.[2] A painting by Francis Hayman dating to about 1750, which has been interpreted as a betrothal portrait, presents this anxiety in a particularly sensitive way (pl.18). Elizabeth Tyers sits close to her father, Jonathan, while her future husband John Wood stands slightly to the side. Elizabeth is stroking the head of a pet dog towards which her father gestures in a graceful allusion to its association with companionship and fidelity. In the background a sculpture of a putto, dove and dolphin signifies the love, peace and long life that a successful marriage could bring.[3]

THE WEDDING

In the eighteenth century most couples married in church. According to church law the service had to take place between eight and twelve in the morning. Before the wedding the couple were required to publish their banns in church on three successive Sundays. The publication of the banns was intended to alert fellow parishioners to the forthcoming wedding so that any illegality could be exposed before the marriage took place. However it was possible to gain exemption from this requirement by buying a licence. Some couples did this to expedite their marriage, others because they felt that publishing their banns was an unwarranted intrusion into their privacy.[4] A small group of people of high rank were entitled to purchase a 'special' licence which permitted the wedding to take place wherever and whenever they wished without the publication of banns. The aristocracy frequently took advantage of this privilege, often marrying in the afternoon or evening instead of the morning, at home or in a church or chapel.[5]

Stephen Beckingham (1697–1756) and Mary Cox (b.1710) married at St Benet's Church at St Paul's Wharf by the river Thames in the City of London. William Hogarth's 1729 marriage portrait of them is a rare eighteenth-century image of a church wedding (pl.19). The sunlight illuminating the spectators watching from above indicates that the ceremony is taking place during the day. The artist depicts the couple at a solemn moment as the groom is about to place the wedding ring on his bride's finger. She wears a formal white silk day dress embellished with gold lace, a lace headdress and sleeve ruffles, and a string of pearls. Her appearance suggests that her family were wealthy. Clothes made of white silk were difficult to keep clean and had limited usefulness, making them a luxury item. Pearls and lace, particularly lace made with metal

threads, were costly. The bridegroom wears a light-coloured coat with silver buttons and matching blue silk waistcoat and breeches. Blue and light colours combined with blue, with silver trimmings, were popular choices for bridegrooms in real life and fiction.[6] The Beckinghams were country gentry and Stephen Beckingham had followed a family tradition of entering the law like his father-in-law.[7] The sober, high-quality clothes of the bridal party reflect their genteel professional background. Most weddings were quiet family occasions and there is nothing unusual in the small number of guests depicted in Hogarth's painting.

PURCHASING THE WEDDING CLOTHES

Depending on the bride's family circumstances several outfits might be purchased for the events associated with the wedding, with the finest and most costly being worn not for the church service but when the bride was presented in public as a wife. This occasion was called the 'appearance'. For middle-class brides this sometimes took the form of a party held at home in the late afternoon or evening

on their wedding day.[8] Brides belonging to the exclusive group of nobles and others of high rank who formed the royal court might also hold a reception after their wedding, but they made their formal appearance as a newly married woman when they were presented to the monarch at court. In 1748, when Mary Browne (d.1773), daughter and heir of William Browne, a physician in King's Lynn in the county of Norfolk, married the London lawyer William Ffolkes (1700–73), 'their remarkable finery' was the talk 'of all the local tea-tables'. The bride wore different outfits for her wedding, for going to church on the first Sunday after her marriage and for her appearance, when she 'received her company'. Barbara Kerrich, wife of the Vicar of Dersingham, took great delight in describing Miss Browne's clothes to her sister. The bride was married in a white satin sack-back dress, 'the apron part' flounced with silver. She wore it with a pink satin petticoat decorated with a band of lace and a deep silver fringe at the hem. On Sunday she wore an outfit made from white corded silk woven with a pattern of green and purple flowers and leaves with tex-

17 *The Marriage Settlement*, William Hogarth (1697–1764), oil on canvas, 1742. The first in a cycle of six moralizing paintings which vividly depict the breakdown of an arranged marriage between the dissolute son of an impoverished earl and a wealthy London merchant's daughter. The earl (far right) and the merchant are haggling over the financial terms of the marriage.
© The National Gallery, London

18 *Jonathan Tyers with his Daughter Elizabeth and her Husband John Wood*, Francis Hayman (1708–76), oil on canvas, c.1750. Elizabeth Tyers' father was the proprietor of London's popular Vauxhall Pleasure Gardens.
Yale Center for British Art, New Haven. Paul Mellon Collection / The Bridgeman Art Library

19 *The Wedding of Stephen Beckingham and Mary Cox*, William Hogarth (1697–1764), oil on canvas, 1729.

Metropolitan Museum of Art, New York / The Bridgeman Art Library

tured silver stalks, and a blue satin petticoat whose seams were overlaid with silver lace. For her appearance she chose a scarlet damask sack-back dress also lavishly trimmed with silver lace. An extravagant display of diamond jewellery and lace accessories completed her outfits.[9] While Barbara Kerrich's letter makes it clear that such magnificence was unusual, and perhaps inappropriate for the locality, the bride was probably guided by the social needs of her future life as the wife of a successful London lawyer.[10]

The most important tradespeople for achieving a modish appearance were the silk mercer, milliner and laceman. Clothing styles changed relatively slowly and until the 1760s the fashionableness of a garment lay in the materials, pattern and colours of its fabric. Following the silk's purchase it was given to a mantuamaker (dressmaker) who cut and constructed the dress and supplied the lining and sewing materials. If the client was unavailable for fitting, an old dress could be used as a model. The cost of a garment lay in the fabric, not the making up. When Lady Jemima Grey married Lord Ashburnham in 1724, the eighteen yards of 'rich silver and white' silk for her wedding dress cost £45 but Elizabeth Ackers, who made the dress, received only

16 shillings.[11] (In 1725 a female servant in London could earn between £6 and £8 a year.[12])

In the latter part of the century, fashion was reflected not just by the choice of fabric but also in the selection and application of trimmings which became the most important element in formal dress. Milliners already dealt in the ribbons, flowers, braids and fringes used to trim dress and they now assumed an important role in the dressmaking process, with many making as well as decorating garments. Mantuamakers and milliners were expected to complete commissions within days. Expensive lace provided the finishing touch to an outfit and headdresses, neckwear and sleeve ruffles were desirable luxury items in a bride's trousseau. Lace's delicate, airy patterns veiled and enhanced the skin and provided a counterpoint to rich and lustrous dress silks. Lady Jemima Grey spent £131 5s 3d on lace before she married. This included a set of Brussels bobbin lace purchased for £40 whose high cost suggests that it was probably chosen to wear at court.[13] Fine whitework embroidery, worked on sheer linen or muslin, was a cheaper alternative.

Most British towns had shops selling dressmaking and sewing materials and tradesmen and women who specialized in making clothes and accessories, but for the latest fashions and most skilful workmanship it was necessary to go to larger towns and cities. Some women enjoyed shopping but shopkeepers regularly waited on clients at home, bringing samples, taking orders and delivering the finished goods. An alternative to personal shopping was to ask friends and relations to act as proxies. When Ellen Tatham put away a fragment of her grandmother's wedding dress from 1769, she ensured that the source of the fabric would not be forgotten by attaching a small note to it, explaining that the silk had been bought in London by cousins of the bride (pl.20). London's shops offered a great variety of home-produced and imported luxury goods and the bride's family evidently thought that the sartorial demands of a public occasion as significant as a wedding could best be met in the capital. The cousins chose a fashionable striped fawn-coloured silk brocaded with small sprays of flowers for the bride.[14]

20 Fragment of brocaded silk, English, 1769. Ellen Tatham saved this fragment of her grandmother's wedding dress, noting that cousins had purchased the fabric in London.
© Manchester City Galleries: Gallery of Costume

ROYAL AND ARISTOCRATIC WEDDINGS

Royal weddings were unique in their splendour and ceremony, and were occasions for great display. The first eighteenth-century British monarch to marry in England was George III (1738–1820) in 1761. His bride was the 17-year-old Princess Charlotte of Mecklenburg-Strelitz (1744–1818) whom he did not meet until her arrival in London on their wedding day (pl.21). Etiquette demanded that foreign-born royal brides discard the clothes of their homeland and Princess Charlotte's trousseau and wedding clothes were prepared for her in London. Her glittering appearance at the evening wedding was recorded by the Duchess of Northumberland, one of the newly appointed ladies of the bedchamber. The bride wore a 'stiff-bodied gown' of silver tissue embroidered and trimmed with silver, and a purple velvet mantle laced with gold and lined with ermine, fastening on the shoulders with large tassels of pearls. Her jewels were magnificent: 'on her Head a little Cap of purple Velvet quite covered with Diamonds, a Diamond Aigrette in the Form of a Crown, 3 dropt Diamond Ear Rings, Diamond Necklace, Diamond Sprigs of Flowers on her Sleeves & to clasp back her Robe, a Diamond Stomacher'.[15] She was accompanied by ten bridesmaids, all daughters of peers, dressed in stiff-bodied gowns of white silk embellished with silver. The king also wore silver

21 *The Marriage of George III*, Joshua Reynolds (1723–92), oil on canvas, 1761. Royal etiquette demanded that foreign brides discard the clothes of their homeland. German-born Princess Charlotte's trousseau and wedding clothes were made in London.

The Royal Collection © 2011 Her Majesty Queen Elizabeth II

22 Portrait of Lady Fanny Montagu, attributed to Charles Jervas (c.1675–1739), oil on canvas, c.1734. Fanny Montagu was a bridesmaid at the marriage of Anne, Princess Royal, and William IV, Prince of Orange, in 1734.

© Christie's Images Ltd 2011

which, like white, is associated with purity. The 'stiff-bodied gown' was an archaic form of dress only worn by female members of the royal family on ceremonial occasions, and at weddings by their bridesmaids. A portrait of Fanny Montagu (d.1788) depicts her in the bridesmaid's dress that she wore at the marriage of Anne, Princess Royal and William IV, Prince of Orange in 1734. It shows the heavily boned bodice, trimmed with lace, petticoat and train which formed this costume (pl.22).

Wedding garments made from white silk woven with metal threads, particularly silver but sometimes gold, were popular with the aristocracy throughout the eighteenth century.[16] The correspondence of Mrs Delany (1700–88), who moved in court circles, includes several references to wedding clothes worn by aristocratic women. She uses the terms 'wedding clothes' and 'bridal apparel' to refer to the gowns worn for the wedding, the private party that followed it and for the bride's presentation at court after her wedding. One wedding ceremony she describes was that of Lady Georgiana Carteret (1716–80), daughter of the 2nd Earl of Granville, to John Spencer (1708–46), brother of Charles, Duke of Marlborough, in February 1733–4. Conducted in a private residence by special licence, the wedding took place between eight and nine at night. Afterwards the bridal party played cards, 'supped at ten, [and] went to bed between twelve and one'. According to Mrs Delany, 'everybody at the wedding was magnificent', with the bride resplendent in 'white satin embroidered with silver, very fine lace; and the jewels the Duchess of Marlborough gave'.[17] It is not clear if the bride's jewellery was given or lent by the Duchess of Marlborough, the bride's new sister-in-law, but either way it expressed her approval of the match and the jewels were a powerful symbol of the lineage and wealth of the family Georgiana had joined. Other letters detail the 'bridal apparel' worn by recently married women for their presentation at court. In 1778 Mrs Delany commented on the lavish use of silver in the bridal clothes of Lady Caroline Dawson (1750–1813) and her magical appearance, 'glittering like the moon in a lympid stream: white and silver, or rather all silver – the

23 Silk satin court dress (front and back), British, 1775–80. This dress was associated by the donor with a wedding. It may have been worn for a very formal private evening ceremony but it is more likely that it was worn for the bride's presentation at court following her marriage.

V&A: T.2&A–1947

prettiest silk I ever saw – and richly trimm'd with silver, festooned and betassel'd'.[18] Silks that incorporated metal threads were prized for the beautiful effects created by light reflecting from their textured surfaces. They were expensive and only the wealthiest could afford them and had occasion to wear them. The royal adoption of silver, and white and silver, for weddings along with its high cost undoubtedly gave the colour combination additional kudos. Commissioning expensive new clothes for court was understood as a mark of respect and allegiance to the crown, and it is likely that women who followed royal precedent and wore white and silver for their presentation as brides did so in the same spirit.[19]

The V&A has two eighteenth-century dresses associated with weddings which are appropriate for wearing at court. One is connected to the marriage of Isabella (b.1716), daughter of William Courtenay,

5th Earl of Devon, who married Dr John Andrew (1711–72) at Exeter Cathedral on 14 May 1744. It is lavishly embroidered with polychrome silks and metal threads, and was undoubtedly prepared for the bride's presentation at court after her marriage.[20] The other, which dates to the late 1770s, is made of pure white silk satin (pl.23). The trained sack-back gown has been skilfully constructed to fit over the wide side hoop that was required for attendance at court and the most formal evening dress, making it suitable for a private evening wedding ceremony with high-status guests and for the bride's presentation at court. It is impossible to verify the dress's provenance but its formality, quality and colour would have made it appropriate for either of these occasions, though it is more likely to have been worn at court. The gown is decorated with undulating chains of large and small puffs of satin, made from broad and narrow strips of fabric gathered to shape and padded with cotton waste. Each puff is edged with delicate silk fly fringe. Fluffy tassels made from the same knotted fringe, which would have fluttered in the slightest draught, are suspended from the bigger puffs.

TWO LONDON WEDDINGS

In the eighteenth century shopkeepers, tradesmen, lower-level professionals and civil servants were described as belonging to 'the middling sort'. They were of a lower social level than high-earning professionals and the merchant class but above the artisan and working class. Laetitia Clark (1741–1801) and David Powell (b. about 1726), who married at St Botolph's Church in Bishopsgate in the City of London on 15 August 1761, came from this background. Laetitia's father was a hatter and her husband dealt in imported Italian goods. Sometime after her wedding Mrs Powell dressed a doll in a replica of her bridal clothes, making the doll's sack-back gown and petticoat from a piece of the silk taffeta which she had chosen for her wedding dress (pl.24). The ivory self-coloured silk was probably woven in Spitalfields in east London, which was an important centre for silk-weaving in Britain. Its design of trailing flowers, which include honeysuckle, roses and carnations, suggests that the silk was designed about five years before Laetitia's wedding. Self-coloured silks dated less quickly than multi-coloured silks with complex designs, and popular patterns were probably stocked by silk mercers for several years.

The dress and petticoat are trimmed with fly fringe and scrolling gathered bands of silk, features typical of the date of Laetitia's wedding. The doll has muslin and thread lace kerchiefs and thread lace triple sleeve ruffles. Her cap is also made of thread lace trimmed with wired silk ribbon. Although the silk Laetitia chose was not the height of fashion her judicious use of trimmings and carefully chosen accessories expressed her awareness of current fashions. As well as making a full set of underwear for the doll, she gave her a glass bead necklace and pinned a spray of artificial myrtle to her bosom. Myrtle and roses have been associated with love and

24 Wax bride doll, London, late 18th century. Laetitia Powell dressed this doll in the same taffeta she wore at her own wedding. It is labelled, 'Mrs Powell wedding suit 1761'.
V&A: W.183: 7–1919.
Gift of Mr H.J. Powell

marriage since the Roman period when they were dedicated to Venus. Both were worn by eighteenth-century brides (pl.25). Although some women may have been unaware of the classical roots of this association, most literate women would have been familiar with the 'language of flowers'.[21] The flowers could be fresh or purchased from a specialist artificial florist.

Sarah Boddicott (1756–90) was a wealthy London merchant's daughter. For her wedding to her second cousin Samuel Tyssen, which took place at

25 *Portrait of Mary Strickland*, unknown artist, oil on canvas, *c*.1742. Mary Strickland (1723–65) paired myrtle and roses when she was painted to celebrate her marriage. Both plants had been associated with love and marriage since Roman times. Daughter of a Roman Catholic counsellor-at-law, she married Michael Blount (1719–92) of Mapledurham in 1742.

St John's Church at Hackney on 28 September 1779, she chose a silk woven in Spitalfields in east London. Its up-to-date pattern of small silver leaves attached to a gently undulating vertical stem is woven in silver strip on a white ground. The delicate linear design reflects the influence of neoclassical taste and is similar to surviving silk patterns woven by the London firm Batchelor, Ham and Perigal.[22] The silk was made into a trained open gown with a fitted bodice and matching petticoat. The petticoat's hem is trimmed with silver fringe headed with silver spangles (sequins) and interspersed with tassels hung with more spangles (pl.26). They, and the spangles worked into the silver lace used to trim the sleeve ends and front facings of the gown's skirt, would have twinkled as the bride moved.

In choosing white and silver Sarah was making a fashionable choice which expressed her taste and her family's means. We do not know if Sarah wore this dress for her wedding or her 'appearance', but its preservation suggests its value to her and her descendants. The dress has been altered and was worn into the 1780s. Five years after their marriage, in 1784, her husband purchased Felix Hall in Essex with an estate of 1400 acres, bringing his family into the landed gentry. Most members of the gentry class were based in the country. Its wealthier members maintained close contacts with London and fashionable society, and they formed a link between the nobility and the local social circles which they led. Less affluent members of the gentry observed the fashions at a distance through better placed relatives, friends and acquaintances.

WEDDING DRESSES OF THE 1770S AND 1780S

A number of British wedding dresses from the 1770s and 1780s survive in museum collections in Britain and the USA. All are made of silk and the most popular colours are cream, pink, and blue and white (pl.27).[23] Several wedding dresses made from light-coloured silks sprigged with flowers, like the silk purchased in London for Ellen Tatham's grandmother in 1769 (pl.20), also survive.[24] Jane Bailey, a wealthy farmer's daughter, chose this style of silk for

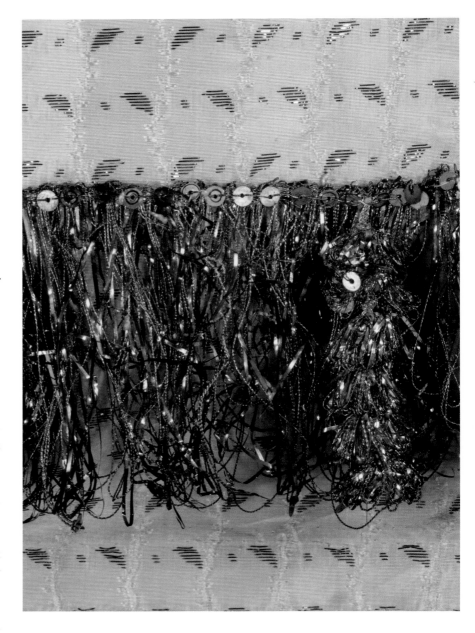

her marriage to James Wickham, which took place at Holy Trinity Church in Wonston, Hampshire on 9 November 1780 (pl.28). The bridegroom was a near neighbour and from the gentry class. The crisp, cream Spitalfields silk of around 1777 has an overall pattern of tiny cream spots. Small circular wreaths enclosing coloured flowers linked by ribbons to floral sprigs, and other smaller floral wreaths are brocaded sparsely into the silk. The bride had the fabric made into a gown and petticoat and she completed her outfit with a modish white silk bergère (shepherdess) hat and white silk shoes. The gown was constructed so that it could be worn in two different forms of the 'polonaise' style. This French fashion, in which the skirt of the gown was drawn up into soft puffs over the petticoat, had been fashionable for about four years. Jane's choice of silk and the style of her dress, which were no longer the peak of fashion, suggest that she wanted to look in tune with current modes, while dressing appropriately for

26 Silk petticoat (detail), British, c.1779, showing the silver tassels and spangled silver fringe on the petticoat's hem.
V&A: T.80A–1948.
Given by Mrs R. Stock

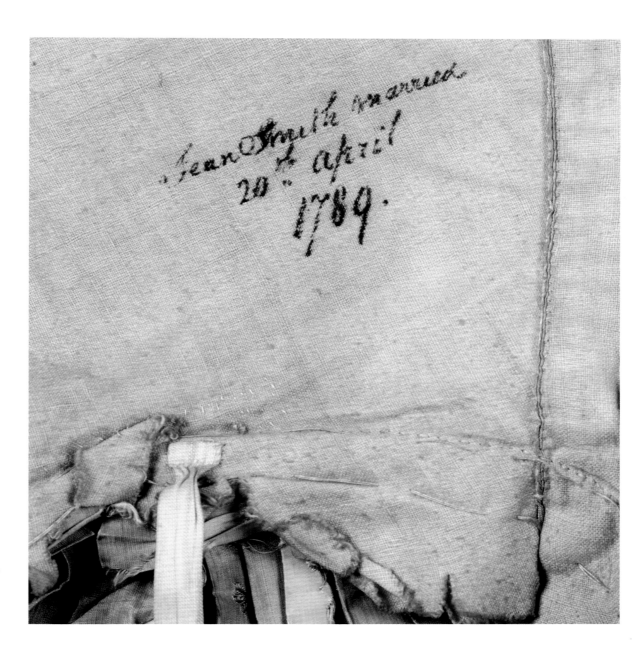

27 Wedding dress
(details below and right),
British, 1789, made from
French or British silk woven
1755–60. This was the first
wedding dress that the
V&A acquired, in 1902.
V&A: 939&A–1902

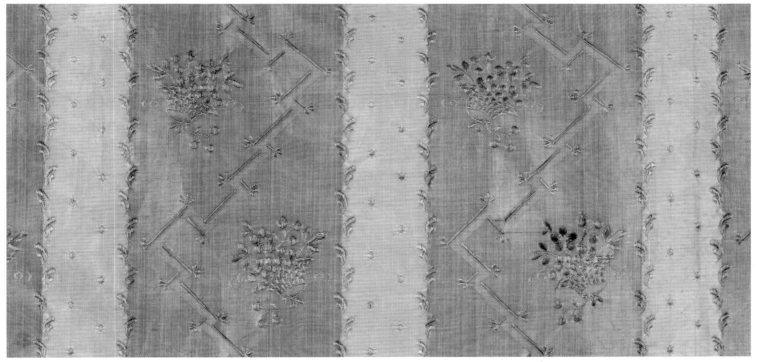

28 Silk gown and petticoat, silk-covered straw bergère hat, and silk satin and leather shoes, British, 1780. Instead of white, Jane Bailey chose to marry in cream-coloured silk brocaded with coloured flowers. The gown could be worn arranged *à la polonaise* (below), a fashionable look of the late 1770s in which the skirt was drawn up into soft puffs over the petticoat.

Photographs by John Chase. Images courtesy of the Olive Matthews Collection, Chertsey Museum

the rural locality where she lived. The pastoral connotations of her kilted skirt and hat certainly made them a romantic choice for a country wedding.[25]

During the 1770s and 1780s fashions in textiles were changing and linen and cotton were taking over from silk. Fine muslin, which was perfectly suited to the new fashion for softer, less restricting styles of dress, was particularly fashionable and in the 1780s it was worn for formal occasions as well as for informal daywear.[26] In 1786 Marianne Clayton (1752–1808) chose silver muslin when she married General Henry Edward Fox (1755–1811) on Valentine's Day. Her gown was trimmed with white satin and she accessorized it with a very fine embroidered muslin apron, a lace-trimmed handkerchief and white and silver shoes. The bridegroom was dressed in 'a dark green coat, with a very pretty waistcoat'. Miss Emelia Clayton and Miss Yates attended her. They were dressed 'exactly alike' in white muslin with handkerchiefs trimmed with lace and blue satin ribbons. This instance of dressing the bride's two attendants in matching clothes is unlikely to have been unique and sets a precedent for the nineteenth-century custom of dressing bridesmaids alike.[27]

Given the limited evidence it is only possible to make generalized statements about the colours women chose for their wedding clothes in the eighteenth century. Contemporary letters and journals are most revealing about the preferences of the aristocracy. Silver, white and silver, and white were the most favoured colours for wedding dresses at this level of society. Most of the surviving dresses in British museums date to the second half of the century. The genealogical research that has been undertaken about their wearers suggests that many came from the gentry and middling classes. Among these women there seems to have been a marked preference for light-coloured silks patterned with flowers and for dresses in pastel colours, either plain or patterned with white. The two groups overlap, with women from the upper gentry, professional and mercantile backgrounds also choosing white and white and silver. Until the 1780s, when muslin became fashionable, silk was the preferred fabric for all.

THE WHITE
WEDDING DRESS

1790–1840

SHRINE of EQUALITY.

Democratic Leveling; __ Alliance a la Françoise; __ or __ The Union of the Coronet & Clyster-pipe.

From the final decade of the eighteenth century through to 1840, when Queen Victoria was married, a white dress gradually became the garment of choice for a well-to-do young woman marrying for the first time. The veil and orange-blossom wreath, with its glossy green leaves and delicate white flowers, were the finishing touches that identified her as a bride. Both became conventional during this period. The fashion for wearing white and silver wedding dresses, which was popular in aristocratic circles in the eighteenth century, did not disappear immediately, but became less popular and by the 1830s white and silver had ceded to white.

Drawing up marriage contracts was still an important preliminary to marriage. The hours when weddings could take place remained the same but in 1837, the year Queen Victoria acceded to the throne, the 1836 Marriage Act and Registration Act came into force. The Marriage Act introduced non-religious civil marriages held in register offices. It also allowed non-conformists and Roman Catholics to be married in their own places of worship. Until this time, unlike Quakers and Jews, they had to marry in Anglican churches. The Registration Act transferred the responsibility for registering births, marriages and deaths from the church to the state.

Fashion magazines and newspapers began to play an important role in promoting the white wedding dress and its accessories. Much of the fashion information published in Britain came from French sources and the history of the relationship between French and British fashion is important to the history of the wedding dress. During the eighteenth century France was admired in Britain for the quality of its silk designs, the creative flair of its milliners and the stylish appearance of its nobility. Britain had its own fashions, particularly for informal and country wear which the French in their turn adapted for themselves, but in general Britain looked to France for fashion innovation and the most up-to-date luxury goods.

This exchange of influence was fed by constant communication between the two countries as people and goods travelled backwards and forwards across the English Channel. But between 1789 and 1814 such an interchange became increasingly difficult due to the French Revolution and subsequent French Wars. The Treaty of Amiens, signed in March 1802, temporarily ended the hostilities between Britain and the French Republic, and prompted a flood of British visitors to Paris to visit friends and relatives and to see and purchase the latest fashions. However after the resumption of the war a year later, Britain remained effectively cut off from France until 1814, when it became possible to visit once more.

FASHIONS AND FABRICS

From 1790 to 1810 white was the dominant colour for women's fashions for informal day and evening wear, and bridal clothes followed suit (pl.29). Horace Walpole noted the trend for white when he described the marriage of Lady Charlotte Bertie (1764–1838) to Lord Cholmondeley (1749–1827) in 1791: 'Well, our wedding is over, very properly, though with little ceremony, for the men were in frocks and white waistcoats, most of the women in white, and no diamonds but on the Duke's wife [the Duchess of Ancaster].'[1] The outfits of the bridal party and particularly the lack of precious jewellery reflected the shift towards a more informal, less ostentatious aesthetic at the end of the century. For women, waistlines began to rise, sleeves were shortened for evening and formal wear and the silhouette gradually became slimmer. Lace accessories such as caps and sleeve ruffles were no longer fashionable, but the prevailing interest in the classical world led to lace veils being draped over the head for evening wear following styles depicted on Greek and Roman artefacts (pl.30). Fine, sheer muslin imported from India was the most fashionable fabric but very light silks, such as gauze, and fine cottons and linens were also popular. Most fabrics were plain with decoration largely limited to woven self stripes, simple embroidery or small printed motifs. Although cartoonists delighted in lampooning the hazards of wearing diaphanously thin fabrics that clung to the body, women wore under-dresses, which might be white or coloured, and, with a few exceptions, corsets for support and propriety.

29 Democratic Leveling;– Alliance a la Française; – or – The Union of the Coronet & Clyster-pipe James Gillray (1757–1815), published 4 March 1796. The etching satirizes the secret wedding of Lady Lucy Rachel Stanhope who eloped, aged 16, with Thomas Taylor, the family apothecary. The bride wears a fashionable white dress and feather-trimmed bonnet decorated with a veil. White was the dominant colour for women's fashions in the 1790s.

National Portrait Gallery, London

Embroidered machine-made net was a fashionable alternative to muslin. The soft sheer fabric draped gracefully and suited the slim columnar silhouette of dresses in the first decade of the nineteenth century. Its use increased after 1809 when John Heathcoat (1783–1861) invented a machine that could produce a durable twisted net closely resembling bobbin-made mesh.

The vogue for muslin was occasionally taken to extremes. Thirty muslin dresses were purchased for Elizabeth Farren's wedding trousseau for her marriage to the recently widowed Lord Derby (1752–1834). The romance between the earl and the charming but reputedly chaste actress Elizabeth Farren (1759–1829) had been a topic of gossip for years and their wedding, which took place on May Day 1797 at Lord Derby's London town house in Grosvenor Square, was widely reported. Eliza de Feuillide, a first cousin of the novelist Jane Austen, wrote derisively of the 'great number of simpletons' from the 'fashionable World' who had 'been to see her Wedding Garments which are superlatively magnificent – She has thirty Muslin dresses each more beautiful than the other, and all trimmed with the most expensive Laces. Her Wedding Night Cap is the same as the Princess Royal's and cost Eighty Guineas – I have no patience with such extravagances, and especially in such a Woman.'[2] Her comment begs the question of where people saw Elizabeth Farren's wedding clothes and who was allowed to see them.

The Times also drew attention to the opportunity and its effect. 'Miss Farren's new wedding dresses have attracted the attention of all the Female Fashionables, and the articles made up for her Use have sold twenty times over. The FARREN is expected to set the fashions for some time to come'.[3] Even allowing for exaggeration, this snippet suggests the commercial possibilities open to an opportunistic dressmaker who supplied wedding clothes for high-profile clients. Whatever Eliza de Feuillide may have thought of the former actress, the new Countess of Derby was known for her elegance and decorum. When she was presented to Queen Charlotte at court following her marriage, she appeared 'in the usual bridal dress of white, remarkably neat but without diamonds, or any other ornaments'.[4] However her wedding night cap costing eighty guineas (£84) was undeniably expensive. When Mary Berry prepared a draft budget for a 'small establishment' around January 1796, she estimated that liveries for three male servants and the coachman would cost £80, while the total annual wages of a housekeeper, a cook, a housemaid and a lady's maid would be £58.[5]

Owning a dressmaking business could be profitable but the women employed in the dress trades often worked under difficult conditions. In December 1806 the wedding of Lady Harriet Villiers (1788–1870) and the Reverend Richard Bagot (1782–1854) was brought to the attention of readers of London's *Morning Chronicle* because of the bravery shown by a dressmaker's assistant who fought off robbers who attacked her as she was delivering Lady Harriet's wedding dress at one thirty in the morning. The wedding took place thirteen hours later at two thirty in the afternoon. The story highlights the long hours dressmakers worked to meet the demands of their clients and the dangers they were expected to accept. The dress, which was made of the 'finest' Indian muslin decorated with lace, had been ordered from Mrs Sowerby, a dressmaker and milliner in New Bond Street whose establishment was located close to the town houses of her aristocratic clients in Mayfair.[6]

Very few wedding dresses survive from the early nineteenth century, but reports in contemporary newspapers sometimes describe the garments worn by notable brides. One of the most widely reported weddings of the period united the heiress Catherine Tylney Long (1789–1825) and William Wellesley-Pole (1788–1857), who adopted the name William Pole-Tylney-Long-Wellesley on their marriage in March 1812 in recognition of the fortune brought by his bride. The couple were married at St James's Church, Piccadilly. The press focused on the bride's wealth, the marriage settlement and her extravagantly expensive wedding outfit. According to the fashion periodical *La Belle Assemblée*, the bride's 'robe of real Brussels point lace' worked in a simple sprig pattern and worn over a white satin under-dress cost seven hundred guineas (£735). This huge sum reflects the expense of the handmade lace. The net ground of Brussels lace was made from narrow strips invisibly joined together, which made large pieces of lace particularly costly and prestigious. The bride completed her outfit with a white pelisse trimmed with swansdown and a Brussels lace bonnet decorated with ostrich feathers and a deep lace veil. The bonnet and its veil were said to have cost one hundred and fifty and two hundred guineas (£157 10s and £210) respectively. By contrast the groom's outfit of a plain blue coat, white waistcoat, buff breeches and white stockings accorded with contemporary ideals of immaculately tailored, elegant, masculine restraint.[7] Comparing the money the bride spent on her outfit with the wages of household servants in London gives some idea of the bride's expenditure on her appearance. In 1811 the 6th Duke of Devonshire, who was a generous employer, paid his butler at Devonshire House £80 a year and junior housemaids up to £16.[8]

From 1813 to about 1825 most wedding dresses illustrated in fashion plates resemble evening dresses with short sleeves and a low décolletage (pl.31). These styles were appropriate for the private ceremonies conducted at home for those eligible to marry by special licence.[9] For church weddings women wore long-sleeved dresses or a pelisse, under which short sleeves could be worn. However it is possible that the fashion plates were used in Britain as a guide to fashionable styles for the trousseau, not just for the wedding dress. As the interest in classical styles waned, dressmakers drew on an eclectic range of sources which encompassed historical and traditional dress. Three-dimensional decoration, adding interest to the sleeves, bodice and hem, became a key feature of fashionable dress at this time. The high waistline, reintroduced in Britain in 1814–15 when it became known that this was how French women were dressing, slowly dropped from 1818, and sleeves and skirts gradually increased in size, creating an hour-glass silhouette.

Many French dressmakers worked in London for British businesses and some ran their own estab-

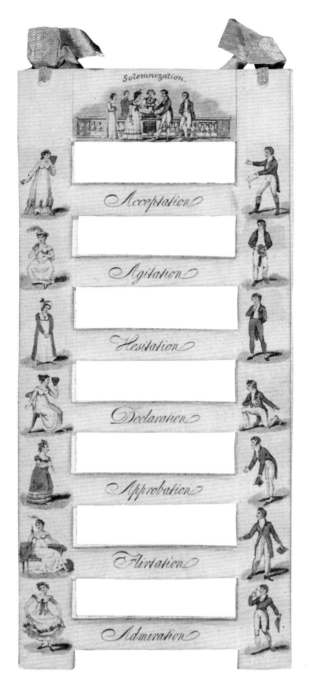

31 The Ladder of Matrimony
published by R. Ackermann,
hand-coloured engraving,
London, 1814–18. At the
'Solemnization', the bride
wears a short-sleeved dress
with low décolletage. The
ladder charts the course of
marriage, from Admiration
up and down to Separation.
V&A: E.2311–1953. Bequeathed by
Guy Tristram Little

lishments.[10] In 1819 Madame Videment drew attention to her bridal dresses in an advertisement, written in cod-French, for her Grand Magazin de Modes in London's Conduit Street, which runs off Bond Street. Her stock included 'un grand ASSOR-TIMENT de BRODERIES of every description, superbes Robes de Mariage, recoit every week an assortment o[f] French Artificial Flowerss, Robes de Bal, Trimmings, and all Novelties'.[11] She claimed to have trained with the celebrated Parisian fashion merchant Louis-Hippolyte LeRoy (1763–1829) who numbered the Empress Joséphine (1763–1814) and many titled British women among his clients.[12] The advertisement stresses the proprietor's seemingly impeccable connections and consequent ability to offer the most up-to-date French luxury goods. A

previous advertisement placed by Madame Videment had been written entirely in French, but perhaps she hoped that a partial translation might reach a wider audience without sacrificing the cachet of her nationality.

FASHION PERIODICALS AND FASHION PLATES

Some women travelled to Paris to buy clothes but most British women learned about French fashions from better-informed friends and relatives, their dressmakers and milliners, who could visit Paris to buy stock and patterns of models for reproduction, and from information published in periodicals and newspapers.[13] British fashion periodicals included lengthy descriptions of French styles illustrated with French fashion plates, originally prepared for a

French readership, and there were English-language versions of French magazines like *Le Follet* (1829–92). The fashion periodicals were targeted as much at dressmakers as at the public, and dressmakers used them to discuss styles with their clients.[14] Regional newspapers reprinted descriptions of the latest fashions from the periodicals, bringing them to a much wider middle-class readership across the country. What women actually wore was informed by these sources, but tempered by constraints such as budget, morality, taste, need and attitudes to dress in their social circle.

The fashion for white wedding dresses was encouraged in France and Britain by descriptions and illustrations of bridal dress which, for the first time, start to appear regularly in fashion periodicals from 1810–19. The earliest known nineteenth-century fashion plate of a bride was published in France in *Le Journal des Dames et des Modes* in 1813. It is unlikely to have been seen by British readers because of the war with France. It depicts the model in a short-sleeved evening dress of embroidered machine net worn over a white silk under-dress. The dress is accessorized with elbow-length gloves, a floral head-dress and lace veil. The rectangular veil, with zigzagged edges, border patterns at the short ends and small motifs scattered over the ground, is draped at the back of the head over a high coiffure and falls to hip height. It is worn with a wreath of roses, and possibly a spray of orange-blossom, and does not cover the face. Both veil and flowers were expressions of fashionable dress, not antiquarian revivals of the Roman bridal veil or the floral wreaths worn over loose undressed hair by sixteenth-century brides.

The earliest known British fashion plate of a bridal gown, published in Rudolph Ackermann's *Repository of Arts, Literature, Commerce, Manufactures, Fashion and Politics* in June 1816, features a dress created by Mrs Gill of Cork Street made of striped French gauze over a white satin slip with short puffed sleeves (pl.32). Its hem is embellished with a deep flounce of Brussels lace. Artificial roses encircle the skirt and rosebuds trim the shallow, low-cut bodice. The model is depicted wearing a diadem over her brow and a spray of pink roses at the back of the head.[15] The *Repository* was published in monthly issues from January 1809 to December 1828 and there were usually two hand-coloured fashion plates in each issue. Although it originally targeted both sexes, after 1816 the balance of contents shifted towards the female reader with an emphasis on light fiction and the arts.[16] Only three issues include images of bridal dress: the example from 1816 and two others published in March 1818 and January 1827. None of the brides in these images has a veil, which suggests that veils were not common in Britain at this time though some women did wear them.

Lady Mary Stanley (1801–58) wore a Brussels lace bridal dress with what one newspaper called a 'superb' matching veil for her wedding to the Earl of Wilton (1799–1882) in December 1821.[17] Veils, which were worn at the back of the head, added interest to the back of the costume and, for all their connotations of chastity, could be very alluring (pl.33). The earliest known fashion plates to show wreaths made from orange-blossom are French and date to 1820.[18] Three years later Mary Elizabeth Williams (1803–89), wore a Brussels lace veil and an orange-blossom wreath when she married George Hammond Lucy (1789–1845) by special licence at St Asaph's Cathedral in Clwyd in north Wales on 2 December 1823. In her memoirs the bride recalled that her new lady's maid dressed her hair and arranged her veil and wreath. Her satin wedding dress survives in the National Trust's collection of dress. Its long-sleeved bodice has applied decoration of stylized leaves and berries (pl.34). Mary Elizabeth Williams had six bridesmaids, four of whom were her sisters. All were dressed in 'simple white cashmere, their bonnets lined with pink', the bride's 'favourite colour'.[19]

From about 1825 to 1835 hair styles were elaborate with curls and ringlets, plaits, buns and knots of hair, and fashion plates were drawn to show how the veil was attached to the hair and its relationship to the headdress. The bride's head is shown reflected in a mirror or face-on and from the side or back (pl.35). By the late 1820s plain tulle veils were fashionable. In 1828 Jean Claude Dognin (1785–1848) of Lyons had produced a very successful machine-

32 '**Bridal Dress**', Rudolph Ackermann's *Repository of Arts, Literature, Commerce, Manufactures, Fashion and Politics*, June 1816. This is the earliest known British fashion plate depicting a bridal gown.

V&A: National Art Library

33 *La Mariée* after Louis Léopold Boilly (1761–1845), lithograph, France, *c*.1820.

Private collection / The Bridgeman Art Library

34 Silk satin wedding dress (detail), British, 1823, worn by Mary Elizabeth Williams when she married George Hammond Lucy. In her memoirs the bride described the colour of her dress as 'snow white'. The silk is now very fragile and appears more cream-coloured.

The National Trust, Killerton House
© NTPL / Andreas von Einsiedal

made silk net dressed with a little stiffening called 'tulle illusion' or 'zephyr', which may have encouraged this trend.[20] Lace scarves with border patterns at both ends were an alternative to veils and by the mid-1830s both extended to the knee and beyond. Bridesmaids and wedding guests also wore veils. Veils were always worn at the back of the head and not over the face in this period.

FROM SILVER AND WHITE TO WHITE

The aristocratic taste for white and silver bridal wear which had dominated the eighteenth century survived into the 1820s. Frances Barrington (1802–49) chose white and silver for her marriage to William Legge, 4th Earl of Dartmouth (1784–1853), which took place in Florence in Italy on 25 October 1828. The wedding was conducted by the bride's father, the Reverend George Barrington, 5th Viscount Barrington of Ardglass (1761–1829) who was living in Italy. Frances Barrington's dress has short, very full sleeves, suggesting that the service was conducted privately. It is made of white silk crêpe threaded with silver strip with a range of surface finishes and decorated with silver spangles (pls 36–7). Although the metal is now tarnished, it is still possible to imagine the beautiful effect that this 'lama' embroidery, as it was known, would have created, with its delicate silver floral sprays on the front of the skirt and sleeves and the bold trail of leaves and berries which sweep round the hem. The bride may have chosen it because dresses decorated with lama were worn for court dress in Britain, France and Italy, making them useful for aristocratic brides. Two recent British royal brides, Princess Mary (1776–1857) and the heir to the throne, Princess Charlotte of Wales (1796–1817), had worn outfits incorporating lama when they married in 1816, continuing yet updating the tradition of silver for royal weddings.[21]

35 'Costume Parisien', *Journal des Dames et des Modes*, 1826. The fashion plate shows how to attach the veil to the elaborate hair style.

Harry Matthews Collection
© Museum of London

36 Silk crêpe wedding dress
embroidered with silver strip
(now tarnished), probably
British or French, 1828. The
dress, in the aristocratic
colours of white and silver, was
altered by its wearer and again,
at a later date, probably for use
as fancy dress.
V&A: T.9–1929. Gift of the Hon. Mrs Brooke

**37 Embroidered silk satin
garters**, British, 1828.
Frances Barrington wore
these garters
on her wedding day.
V&A: T.9A, B–1929. Gift of the
Hon. Mrs Brooke

Eliza Larken (1807–63) also married in 1828 (pl.38). She was the daughter of Edmund Larken, an administrator with the East India Company. For her wedding to William (later 6th Baron) Monson (1796–1863), which took place at St Giles-in-the-Fields Church in London, Eliza Larken ordered a short-sleeved dress with a separate pair of long sleeves which fit so neatly over the integral sleeves that they need only one hook and eye to keep them in place. The dress is made from a crisp white striped cream silk, figured with small floral sprigs, and trimmed with pale gold and white satin and hand-made blonde silk lace. For her wedding she would have worn the dress with its long sleeves and matching pelerine (a long, shaped scarf). Without the sleeves it would be suitable for formal afternoon and evening wear (pl.39). The versatility exemplified by this wedding outfit is a feature of nineteenth-century dress and reflects an economical approach that was considered a virtue. Remarkably the headdress Eliza wore for the wedding has also survived. It is a net cap trimmed with lace supported on a satin-covered frame shaped to accommodate the bride's curls and ringlets. The frame is decorated at the front with tiny cut steel beads and a row of opalescent shells.

**38 *Eliza, wife of the 6th
Baron Monson*,** William
Egley (1798–1870),
watercolour on ivory, c.1828.
Private collection

39 Silk wedding dress, over-sleeves and pelerine trimmed with blond silk lace, British, 1828. Eliza Larken wore the dress like this for her marriage to William (later 6th Baron) Monson (left). It could also be worn without its detachable over-sleeves and pelerine as an evening dress (right).

V&A: T.124:1,2–2009; T.374:1,2–2009

40 'Wedding Dress',
Costumes Parisiens, 1831.
Unlike many surviving
wedding dresses of the time,
those depicted in fashion
plates in the 1830s have
increasingly elaborate
trimmings.
Bibliothèque des Arts Decoratifs,
Paris / Archives Charmet /
The Bridgeman Art Library

**41 Muslin and silk pelisse-
robe**, British, 1834.
Embroidered muslin collar,
British, 1830–40. This dress
is associated with a wedding
in the Mayo family, probably
that of Herbert Mayo (b.1798)
and Mary-Anne-Grace Quin
who married at St Mary's
Church, Stoke Newington,
London on 3 November 1834.
The dress was donated to the
V&A with the wedding dress
worn by their daughter
Anne-Katharine Mayo for her
marriage in 1869.
V&A: T.63–1973: Gift of Miss Gaster.
T.114–1973: Given by Miss S. Cowdell

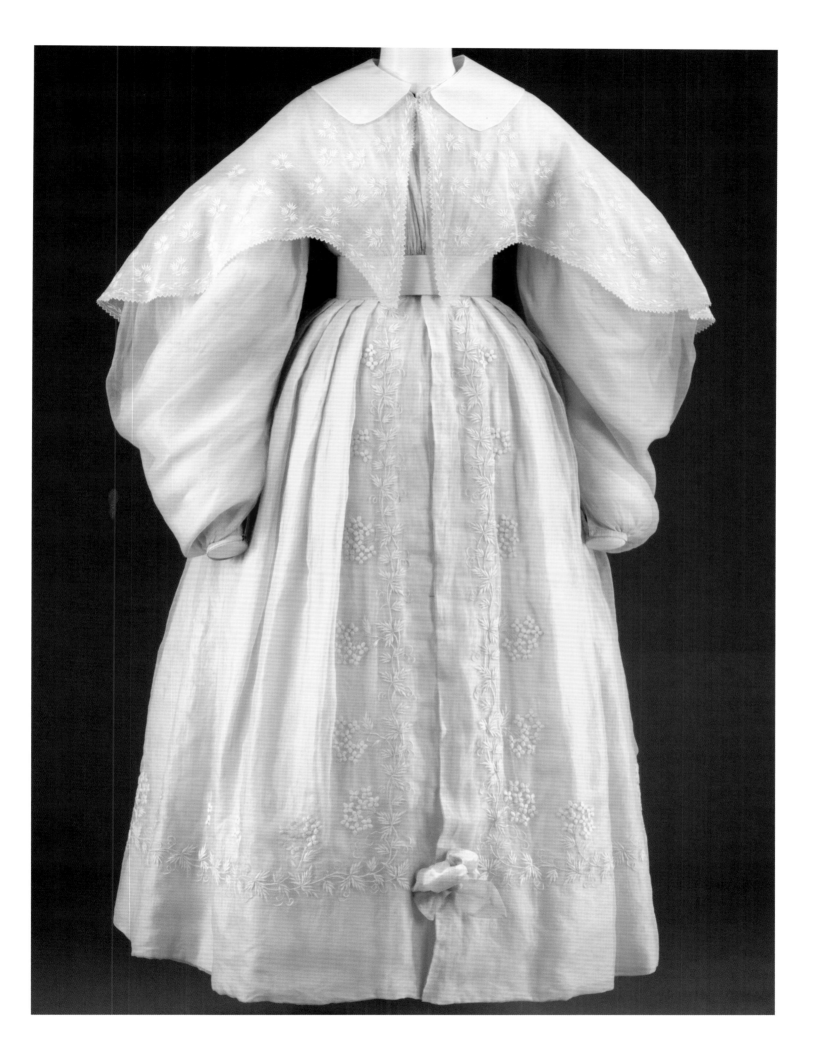

42 Muslin and silk pelisse-robe (details)
V&A: T.63–1973: Gift of Miss Gaster.
T.114–1973: Given by Miss S. Cowdell

In the early 1830s bridal dresses described in fashion periodicals tend to have increasingly elaborate trimmings, with falls of lace at the neck and over the sleeves, frills and bows, and flounces decorating the hemline (pl.40). Surviving dresses often demonstrate a more restrained approach to decorative trends. The V&A collection includes a graceful pelisse-robe probably worn by Mary-Anne-Grace Quin for her marriage in 1834, made from white muslin set over white silk (pls 41–2). It is simply but skilfully embroidered in white with trailing leaves, tendrils and clusters of flowers, and has a single bow placed just above the hem at the centre front. It would probably have been accessorized with a collar and pelerine, bonnet and wrist-length gloves (pl.43). Bonnets remained a popular alternative to veils for church weddings. They were an everyday accessory that could be retrimmed after the wedding to extend their use.

The marriage of Queen Victoria (1819–1901) to Prince Albert of Saxe-Coburg and Gotha (1819–61) on 10 February 1840 was a defining moment in the history of the white wedding dress in Britain. After considering the precedents set by earlier royal brides, such as Princess Charlotte of Mecklenberg-Strelitz who wore silver tissue for her wedding in 1761 (p.28), the twenty-year-old queen decided to make her marriage vows to her 'precious Angel' as his future wife rather than as the monarch. She wore a creamy-white silk satin court dress embellished with lace, choosing Spitalfields silk from London and Honiton lace made in Devon to demonstrate her support for British manufactures. Instead of wearing the crimson velvet robe of state, she opted for a white satin court train bordered with sprays of orange-blossom, and in place of a circlet, she wore a deep wreath of artificial orange-blossom with a Honiton lace veil pinned to the back of her head.

43 'The Bridesmaid, The Bride', *La Belle Assemblée*, September 1832. Some brides wore bonnets and bonnet veils in preference to bridal veils. Bonnets were more useful than veils because they were an everyday accessory that could be worn on many occasions.

V&A: E.2844–1888

44 *The Orange Blossom*, c.1848. The title of this song and the image used on its cover show how closely associated the veil and orange-blossom had become with bridal attire by the mid-nineteenth century.

Spellman Collection of Victorian Music Covers, University of Reading

THE ORANGE BLOSSOM.

Twelve daughters of peers, also in white silk but with white roses decorating their hair and their dresses, acted as trainbearers. George Hayter's painting of the royal wedding emphasizes the delicate femininity of the bridal group and aptly conveys the visual and emotional impact of their massed white dresses (pl.45).

Orange-blossom was prized for its fragrance and was a symbol of virtue and fertility. Although orange trees were grown in England, most brides purchased artificial flowers, made from wax, stiffened cotton or paper. Mr Rogers of Eaton Square supplied the orange-blossom for Queen Victoria's

45 The Marriage of Queen Victoria and Prince Albert, 10 February 1840,
George Hayter (1792–1871), oil on canvas, 1840–42.

The Royal Collection © 2011
Her Majesty Queen Elizabeth II

wedding and Mrs Peachey, a specialist in wax modelling, supplied the wedding favours, which combined white roses, orange-blossom and myrtle tied with white satin ribbon.[22] In her book on wax flower modelling Mrs Peachey drew attention to the problem of wax flowers wilting in the heat of crowded rooms and sticking to the hair. She recommended attaching a fine wire half way up the back of each petal and sprinkling white flowers with her preparatory arrow-root. Coloured flowers were protected by the paint used to colour the wax. Stems were wrapped in narrow ribbons to which scent could be applied.[23]

Details of Queen Victoria's appearance at her wedding were disseminated throughout the country in newspaper reports, cheap prints and souvenirs. This publicity reinforced the notion that a wedding dress should be white and worn with a veil and orange-blossom. On Valentine cards and sheet music covers (pl.44) this is what brides wear, although in reality coloured dresses were common. Queen Victoria's decision to wear a white wedding dress made it desirable at all levels of society and a symbol of romantic love and purity. For brides who could afford white, and who were marrying for the first time, a white wedding dress became the norm.

A working-class wedding

This modest block-printed cotton day dress is the earliest documented working-class wedding dress in the V&A collection (pl.46). It was worn by Sarah Maria Wright (1817–1908) for her marriage to a farm labourer, Daniel Neal (1816–1907) at St Nicholas's Church in Skirbeck, Lincolnshire, on 27 July 1841.

Although made in 1841, Sarah's dress, with its high waist and full gathered sleeves and skirt, reflects an earlier fashionable silhouette of the mid- to late-1830s. Fashion plates show that 1838–41 was a transitional period during which full sleeves and short-waisted bodices gave way to a slimmer, elongated silhouette. The new style is exemplified by an extremely fashionable cream silk gown also worn in 1841, by an unknown bride (pl.47). Its tightly fitted, long-waisted bodice and narrower sleeves mark out its urbane sophistication. Although in contrast Sarah's dress illustrates the delay between the introduction of new fashions and their filtering down to rural communities who would not have had ready access to the latest fashion news, it would still have been considered a smart day dress.

Despite the slightly dated styling, Sarah's dress is made from a fashionable cotton block-printed with an abstract design. The ribbons were probably printed using an ombré block, which creates a soft gradation of tone. The printed fabric may be an example of the use of the toby tub, which made it possible to print several colours at once, instead of printing each colour separately. This labour-saving technique would have reduced the costs of the print, making this up-to-date fabric more affordable to a working-class bride. The fabric reflects the height of fashion for spring 1840, when ombré designs were beginning to be popular, and the fabric would have remained smart and fashionable for several years after the wedding.[1]

We do not know how Sarah acquired the fabric. Skirbeck is over twenty miles from Lincoln – a long journey to make to buy the material from a shop. She may have purchased it from a pedlar. Itinerant salespeople catered to people in remote rural areas who were unable to travel easily to the nearest town or city. Their wares typically included haberdashery goods and dress fabrics, trinkets and small useful household objects including sponges, scissors and kitchen utensils.

A washable cotton fabric in a colourful print was a sensible choice, giving the dress potential for a long and useful life. Many working-class wedding dresses were worn for Sunday best, altered and remade to extend their life as long as

46 Cotton wedding dress, British, 1841.
V&A: T.27–2006. Given by Sheila Battram and Linda Grantham

47 Figured silk satin wedding dress trimmed with tulle, British, 1841.
V&A: T.17–1920.
Gift of Miss H. Bousfield

possible. They were worn until they wore out, so Sarah's dress is a rare survival, though it too shows signs of reuse. At one point the bodice was neatly enlarged in the back, most likely to accommodate the early stages of pregnancy.

After their wedding, Sarah and Daniel Neal went to live at Woad Farm House in Skirbeck, where Daniel probably assisted with the production of woad. Woad, which produced an indigo blue dye, was grown and processed at Skirbeck until 1932, when the last woad mill in Britain closed down.[2]

Daniel Milford-Cottam

COMMERCIALIZING
THE WHITE WEDDING

1840–1914

During the reign of Queen Victoria the white wedding dress, veil and orange-blossom wreath (pls 48–9) became traditional rather than merely fashionable. However the key elements of this tradition – dress, veil, headdress and, from the 1840s, bouquet – remained subject to fashionable change. The invention of photography made it possible from the 1840s to produce an exact image of how the bride and groom looked in their wedding clothes, and, following the introduction of the carte-de-visite in the late 1850s, to distribute multiple copies for personal, political and commercial purposes. Photographs of brides can be compared with fashion plates to assess how long fashions remained popular and, if the wedding was reported in the press, compared with written descriptions of the bride's outfit.

The reigns of Victoria (1837–1901) and her son Edward VII (1901–10) were politically and economically turbulent but the privileged lifestyle of fashionable society, which was dominated by the aristocracy and wealthy upper classes, remained largely unchanged. This chapter focuses on the weddings of women who moved in these circles up to the outbreak of the First World War in 1914. Wealthy brides benefited from the Married Woman's Property Acts of 1870 and 1882, which gave a wife the right to own, buy and sell her separate property and keep her earnings. This made marriage contracts unnecessary for many couples, removing one of the most stressful aspects of the betrothal period.[1] Another popular piece of legislation was a bill enacted in 1886 which extended the hours when a marriage could be solemnized from noon until three o'clock in the afternoon, making early afternoon weddings followed by a tea-party fashionable.

WEDDINGS IN FASHIONABLE SOCIETY

Aristocratic weddings had been reported in newspapers since the eighteenth century but accounts of high-profile weddings become more detailed and frequent in the Victorian period. Although members of the aristocracy were entitled by special licence to marry in private, from the mid-nineteenth century they increasingly chose to marry in public, in church, after the publication of banns. This shift has been attributed to the heightened religious atmosphere generated by the Oxford Movement, whose members wanted to reform and reinvigorate the Church of England and ensure its independence from the state. Launched in 1833, the movement had a long-term influence on the theory and practice of Anglicanism and infused it with greater spiritual fervour. It resulted in the establishment of Anglican religious orders and the reintroduction of some Catholic rites into church services.

The new emphasis on ritual, particularly on the service of Holy Communion, and the desire to enhance the spiritual experience of the congregation led to a general move in the Church of England to beautify the interiors of its churches and expand their capacity and functionality. This made churches much more attractive and convenient for weddings and may have been a contributory factor in the shift in aristocratic practice. At St James's Piccadilly, one of most popular churches for upper-class weddings, access and circulation were improved and seating increased, making the church suitable for larger congregations. The organ was restored, enhancing its musical reputation, and from 1846 a series of stained glass windows were installed, adding atmosphere and colour. In 1866 the gas lights were changed to throw light mainly from the ceiling, improving lighting and air circulation. Similar improvements were carried out in churches across the country. The provision of vestries, which did not exist in many churches, and expansion of chancels were particularly important. They made it possible to sign the registry in private in the vestry and have a full choral service. Music became an increasingly important part of the wedding service after its introduction around 1850.

John Cordy Jeaffreson, who published a history of weddings in 1872, drew attention to the new aristocratic preference for church weddings. He cited religious sentiment as a reason but argued that reluctance to pay for a special licence as well as the now obligatory honeymoon, and women's 'love of picturesque ostentation' were also responsible.[2] Display and performance certainly played a role in upper-class weddings but they were not driven simply by a desire to show off. Marriages played a key

role in reinforcing the exclusivity and privilege of the upper classes. The changes in society caused by industrialization increased the prosperity of the middle class and created a body of very wealthy men from diverse social backgrounds. This generated concerns among the established upper classes about maintaining social distinctions and led to the concept of what its members termed 'society'. This social grouping was not static or impermeable, but admission was carefully controlled and those with the wealth and aspiration to join had to be invited. The marriage market was particularly important to society as it enabled it to retain its exclusivity while absorbing new families whose children were deemed to be suitable matches. Parents did not actively arrange marriages but they went to considerable efforts to control their children's social lives so that they met the 'right' people. The subsequent weddings were often occasions of great pomp and spectacle which demonstrated the wealth and sta-

tus of the families they united and by implication the strength of society as a social unit.[3]

The wedding of Georgiana Dawson Damer (1826–66) to Viscount Ebrington (1818–1905) is a good example of a society wedding which, like many, was reported in the press. The event received detailed coverage in *The Belfast News-Letter*, as the Damers had Irish links and the wedding was potentially interesting to an Irish readership.[4] The wedding took place on 18 March 1847 at Came Church, near Weymouth on the south coast of Britain. The bride lived at Came House, a substantial mid-eighteenth-century house with a classical façade, and at eleven o'clock she, her ten bridesmaids and members of her and the groom's family walked in procession to the church. This was a common practice at country weddings, but unusual for a wedding whose guests included Prince Louis Napoleon of France and 'the *elite* of rank, beauty and fashion', who drew a large crowd of spectators to the event.

49 *Changing Homes*, George Elgar Hicks (1824–1914), oil on canvas, 1862. Hicks's sentimental portrait shows the now traditional white wedding dress, worn with a veil and orange-blossom. Men's dress became darker and more uniform in the 1860s.

© The Geffrye Museum, London / The Bridgeman Art Library

50 Honiton lace wedding veil (detail), British, *c*.1850. This veil was probably worn by a wealthy middle-class bride. Its pattern includes pea-pods, which are symbols of fruitfulness and happiness.
V&A: T.110–1968.
Given by Miss O. Matthews

In the procession the bride and her father were preceded by six child bridesmaids, dressed in white muslin and pink jackets trimmed with swansdown, and followed by four older bridesmaids, also dressed in white muslin, with pink scarves and sashes and white bonnets trimmed with pink roses. The bride, who was commended for her 'chaste and elegant' appearance, wore an 'exceedingly white' watered glacé silk dress, trimmed with three deep flounces of Honiton lace, a Honiton lace veil and orange- flower wreath. Queen Victoria's patronage of the Honiton lace industry encouraged other wealthy brides to follow her example and provided a welcome stimulus to the trade (pl.50). When the newlyweds left the church twenty-four girls from Mrs Damer's charity school scattered flowers in their path.

The trappings of fashionable weddings and the contrast between the poverty of those who gathered outside the church and the wealth and extravagance of those within were the subject of satire. A 'Panorama of a Fashionable Wedding' (pl.51), published in *The Illustrated London News* in 1855, was arranged in processional form, starting with 'The Lovely Bride (Smothered in hysterics and Honiton lace)' and moving on to 'The Twelve Bridesmaids', 'The Charity Children singing their best in expectation of buns and wine', 'The Faithful Servants and Interested Tradesmen, some [of] whom strew flowers before the Lovely Bride' and finally 'The Mob'.[5] It is unclear whether the tradesmen were offering thanks for services rendered or were fawning over the bridal party in hope and anticipation. Weddings were certainly a market worth exploiting and their commodification was reflected in the number of businesses advertising goods associated with them. These range from stationers, photographers, caterers and confectioners to jewellers, florists and suppliers of fabric and dress. A similar cartoon of 1861 in the society magazine *The Queen* compared a fictional high-society wedding, which joined a peer's

PANORAMA OF A FASHIONABLE WEDDING.

The Lovely Bride, (Smothered in hysterics an Honiton lace).   The Rt. Rev. Father, &c., the Bishop.   Three Rt. Revs, who assisted the Rt. Rev. Father, &c.   Three Parsons' Clerks who assisted the &c.   The Duke who gave away the Bride.

The Small German (with a Principality as big as Mecklenburg-square), who has honoured the ceremony with his presence.   The Mother of the "Lovely Bride," &c. (In tears of course).   The Father, in emotion and dress tights.   The Twelve Bridesmaids, who waited on the Lovely Bride.   The Lady's Maid, with Scent-bottles, Preston Salts, Eau de Cologne, and other Restoratives.

The Young Member of Parliament, who is reported to have been rejected, and who attends to prove that he was not.   The Old Nurse (who recollects the Lovely Bride when she was only so high—bless her!   The Rosy Beadle, who is always getting in the way of everybody, and always crying out "Silence."   The Two Smiling Pew Openers, who make so bold, &c.   The Relations (all of whom have carriages).

The Bosom Friends And Loving Acquaintances, looking down (and criticising) from the Gallery.   The Organist, and the Signor, and the Madame, and the Singing Master, who have kindly given their services on this occasion.   The Charity Children singing their best in expectation of buns and wine.

The Faithful Servants and Interested Tradesmen, some of whom strew flowers before the Lovely Bride.   The Powdered Footmen with their Bamboos, Nosegays, Favours, and pink calves.   The Postboys who have been drinking the Young Missus's Health all the morning.   The Poor Bridegroom (inset) looking extremely sleepy, as if he had never been up so early before

The Mob—who have been attracted by the show of highly-emblazoned coachmen and carriages outside.

52 Silk waistcoat, British, 1848. The embroidered lilies of the valley and forget-me-nots were symbols associated with love and purity of heart.
V&A: T.562–1919. Given by Francis C. Eeles

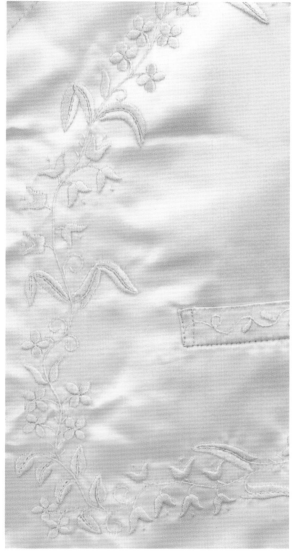

51 'Panorama of a Fashionable Wedding', *The Illustrated London News*, 20 October 1855. The panorama includes the bride 'smothered in hysterics and Honiton lace'.
V&A: National Art Library

daughter with the son of a recently ennobled financier, with those of the London poor.[6]

The standard of living of the middle classes rose in the nineteenth century and some middle-class families aspired or felt pressured to emulate the upper classes. In 1870 a letter to the editor of the *Pall Mall Gazette* reflected on the folly of the middle classes aspiring to ape the practices of high society: 'that middle-class fathers, struggling against increased prices and increased taxation, should give way to such extravagance is one of the weaknesses of the age ... As in the case of expensive funerals, so in the case of costly marriages, money is wasted at the very time when it is most wanted.'[7] The tone is slightly tongue-in-cheek and the letter may be fictional, but the humour makes a serious editorial point about a real social concern.

THE BRIDEGROOM

More weight has been given to bridegroom's clothes in this chapter because the number of garments that survive from the mid-nineteenth century is significantly higher than for other periods. Contemporary writing and advertisements suggest that it was becoming customary for men to purchase new clothes for their weddings in the mid-nineteenth century. These sources and the surviving clothes suggest that commerce and sentiment encouraged this change in practice. Some men selected wedding garments decorated with motifs associated with love. In 1848 a Mr Eeles bought a white satin waistcoat embroidered with lilies of the valley and forget-me-nots for his wedding (pl.52). In the language of flowers the former signify purity of heart and the latter true love. Mr Eeles kept his waistcoat with his

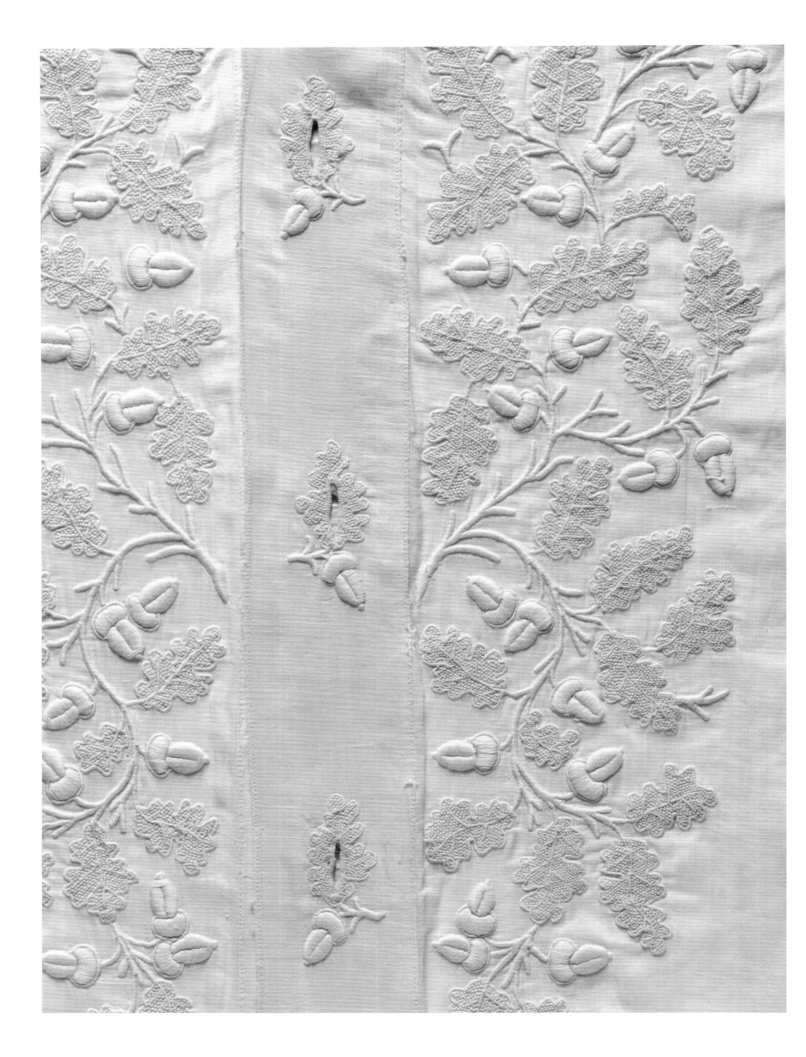

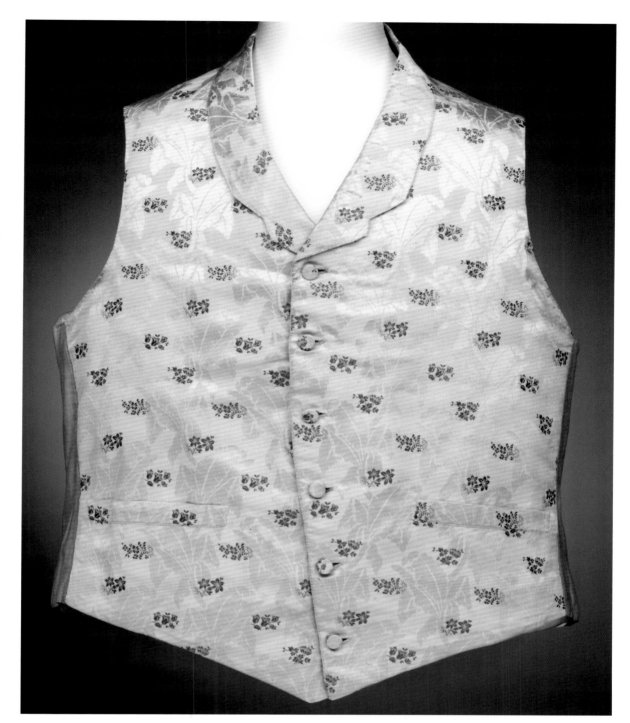

53 Embroidered wedding shirt (detail), British, 1848. This cotton fragment is embroidered with oak leaves and acorns, symbols of love's strength.

V&A: T.147–1925.
Given by Mrs Herbert Terry

54 Figured silk waistcoat, British, 1853. Waistcoats are the most common surviving male garments associated with weddings.

V&A: T.121–1949.
Given by Miss C.M. Higgs

wedding shirt, which has an inset muslin front finely embroidered in white cotton with trefoils. White on white embroidery was used to decorate the wedding shirt worn by Edward Morley Perkins (b. about 1822), an ironmaster and coal owner living in London, who married Octavia Shuter (b. about 1827) on 9 November 1848.[8] Only a torn fragment survives but it is enough to show the pattern of oak leaves and acorns chosen by the bridegroom and its skilful workmanship (pl.53). In the context of weddings, oak is emblematic of the strength of love.

Publications about men's fashion do not suggest that any special clothes should be worn for weddings. The etiquette was to wear formal daywear unless the bridegroom was serving in the military or, like Prince Albert, held a military rank, when dress uniform could be worn. However men's outfitters who supplied middle-class men with ready-made and made-to-measure clothes advertised wedding waistcoats and suits. Waistcoats are the most common surviving male garments associated with weddings. In 1853 George Higgs (1826–1925) chose a waistcoat of white silk damask with a ground pattern of leaves scattered with small sprays of green flowers for his marriage to Ann Smith Corderoy (b.1829) on 12 July (pl.54). Higgs was a civil servant employed in the Admiralty in London and, like his wife, a Methodist. Five years later George Knight spent £6 7s on wedding clothes at Walter Ray Jones, a men's outfitter in Cannon Street in the commercial heart of London. Knight's choice of a blue wool frock coat, lavender tweed trousers and a white and cream silk waistcoat reflects his interest in his appearance and the desire to mark the occasion of his marriage by wearing new clothes.[9] Advertisements for wedding waistcoats suggest that while his waistcoat, which cost £1 4s, was from the top of the range, his coat and trousers were more modest acquisitions.[10] These prices can be put in context by comparing them with servants' wages. In the late 1850s the wife of the Member of Parliament Benjamin Disraeli gave their highest paid domestic servant, the butler, £60 a year while the housemaid earned £14.[11]

Higher up the social scale, Lord Skelmersdale's (1837–98) wish to look his best for his bride Lady Alice Villiers (1841–97) amused his future father-in-law Lord Clarendon. Preparing for his marriage in 1860, the young man ran 'in and out of the house all day like a great Newfoundland puppy . . . yesterday he brought a pocket full of patterns as he wished Alice to select the color of the trowsers in wh[ich] : he sh[oul]d: attend her wedding & he said *everything* he had on w[oul]d: be new & worn for the first time on that day'. Lord Clarendon's comment that he was 'awfully cracky' (crazy) suggests that consulting the bride and buying a new set of clothes was alien to his generation.[12] Lord Skelmersdale undoubtedly patronized a Savile Row tailor employing highly skilled cutters who made precisely fitted, custom-made garments from the finest cloth. From the early 1860s men's clothes became more uniform and darker coloured and many grooms now adopted the standard garb of a dark grey or black coat worn with lighter trousers and a white waistcoat (pls 48–9).

ROYAL WEDDINGS AND BRIDAL FASHIONS
British and European royal weddings continued to excite public interest, and elements of the styles worn by royal brides filtered down into wedding fashions. In 1853 columns of newsprint were dedicated to the marriage of Napoleon III of France (1808–73) and Eugenia de Montijo de Guzmán

(1826–1920). The bride, who was of Spanish-Scottish descent, was good-looking and stylish. With the encouragement of her husband, who recognized the economic value of her support for the French luxury trades, she quickly became an influential leader of fashion, numbering Queen Victoria among her many female admirers. The illustrated papers supplemented reports of her trousseau and wedding clothes with line engravings (pl.55). In London, Madame Tussaud's waxworks exhibited a tableau of the 'nuptial group' in which the Empress was presented in a replica of the dress she wore for the religious ceremony, offering the paying public in London another way of seeing what the Empress wore.[13] The essential elements of her outfit – a bodice extending into a basque and full flounced skirt – were popular for weddings for another five years (pl.56), though few could afford the Brussels lace ruffles, flounces and full-length veil that distinguished the new Empress's costume.

The cut of the Empress's outfit is reflected in the silk day dress which Margaret Scott Lang (d.1915) chose for her marriage to Henry Scott (1827–62) of Bombay (Mumbai) at the Marylebone Presbyterian Church in London on 24 February 1857. Her husband's occupation is unknown, but many men of Scottish origin worked in the civil service in India. Margaret's dress has a jacket-style bodice with a cape and basque finished with silk fringe and low-set, elbow-length sleeves gathered into puffs over the upper arm above wide fringed cuffs (pl.57). Its voluminous skirt, which falls in three deep fringed flounces, is lined and faced with buckram for stiffness. The dress was ordered with a matching low-cut bodice so that the skirt could also be used for evening dress. This was a common practice. It is made of fine ivory silk figured with a pattern of roses and its delicate femininity is typical of its period. The bride may have ordered buckram because she did not want to wear a cage crinoline with such fine silk, preferring to support her skirt with starched flounced petticoats to create the fashionable volume without compromising the appearance of the fabric. The orange-blossom wreath which survives with the dress suggests that it was worn with a veil.

55 'The Empress of the French, in her Bridal Costume', *The Illustrated London News*, 5 March 1853. The marriage of Napoleon III of France and Eugenia de Montijo de Guzmán was widely reported in the British press.

Though lace and tulle veils attached to the back of the head remained fashionable, in the late 1850s some brides chose to wear a tulle veil drawn down over their face and upper body. This new style was described in French fashion magazines as *à l'espagnole* (in the Spanish style), *à la paysanne* (in peasant style), *à la hongroise* (in the Hungarian style) and *à la juive* (in the Jewish style). The variety of terms, particularly the romantic but generic 'peasant style', suggests that this innovation was fashion-led. However the reference to Jewish custom, in which the bridal veil connotes chastity and modesty, reflects the aura of purity that the gossamer fine tulle cast around the bride. The veil also protected the bride from the public gaze, concealing any shyness or tears. French fashion writers thought that plain tulle was more appropriate than lace for young brides, lending a 'poetic charm' to their appearance.[14] The style can be seen in a photograph of a wedding which was preserved among a collection of Victorian Valentine cards (pl.58). (While it appears to have been taken during the ceremony, lighting in churches was too poor for photography and the photograph was probably staged.)

The invention of carte-de-visite photographs (so-called because they were similar in size to visiting cards) introduced a new way of disseminating images. Available in Britain from the late 1850s, these small photographs were produced in multiples from a single photographic plate and mounted on cards, making them ideal gifts. In a reputable studio they cost between half a guinea and a guinea (£1 1s)

JOURNAL DES JEUNES PERSONNES

27ME ANNÉE

Modes
Toilettes d'Hiver.

1858.

Bureaux de l'Administration, 88, rue de Richelieu.

56 'Toilettes d'Hiver', *Journal des Jeunes Personnes*, 1858. Flounced skirts for wedding dresses remained fashionable throughout the 1850s.
V&A: E.22396 (327)–1957.
Given by the House of Worth

57 Silk wedding dress (jacket bodice and skirt) with replica collar, British, 1857. The bride would have worn detachable wrist-length muslin under-sleeves for her wedding.
V&A: T.10A, C–1970.
Given by the Misses I. & N. Turner

for twelve, but peripatetic photographers charged less. In London the number of photographic studios increased from sixty-six in 1855 to two hundred and eighty-four in 1866, with forty in Regent Street alone, the capital's most fashionable shopping destination.[15] In 1859 the stationers Papeterie Marion in Regent Street offered photographs of the 'Happy Pair' taken by (George) Herbert Watkins (b.1828) to be mounted as miniatures in 'two elaborately ornamented escutcheons, surrounded by orange flower blossoms and love knots stamped in silver'.[16] The souvenirs were designed as keepsakes to be pre-

served. Messrs Marion were also the agent for the American photographer John Mayall (1813–1901) who took photographs for Queen Victoria. In 1863 the queen commissioned him to photograph her son Edward, Prince of Wales (1841–1910) and Princess Alexandra (1844–1925) in their wedding clothes (pl.59). The photographs were issued as cartes-de-visite for sale to the public. For the royal family the cartes-de-visite promoted a positive image of the future king as a family man and introduced his Danish bride to the public in an intimate format, encouraging loyalty to the crown. Mrs James, one of London's leading dressmakers, made the princess's white satin wedding dress. The dress was lavishly trimmed with orange-blossom and Honiton lace made with a design of roses, thistles and shamrocks (representing England, Scotland and Ireland) cascading from horns of plenty. The princess's appearance prompted her husband to compare her to a 'Rustic Goddess'.[17]

Mrs James also prepared the wedding clothes for Christina Campbell Cameron (b.1846), who wed Henry Spencer Lucy (1830–90) on 5 July 1865. The couple visited the dressmaker with the groom's mother, Mary (see p.45), to choose the bride's wedding clothes. Mrs James played on her royal

connections, and her charm and gushing enthusiasm for dressing the bride made it 'difficult to say no to anything she recommended', resulting in bills of alarming size. The bride wore a dress 'of the richest white silk, covered with the most exquisite tunic of Brussels lace looped up at the front with large bunches of orange flowers and true-lovers' knots of white satin'. According to Mary Lucy, she looked 'perfect'. Mrs James herself attended the bride and 'acted as lady's maid … so that every fold sat in its right place'.[18] Such personal attention was reserved for important or very favoured clients. Trimming wedding dresses with sprays and swags of orange-blossom, which became particularly popular in the 1870s, made the white wedding dress more specifically bridal. In Britain it distinguished the wedding gown from the white court presentation dress worn by young women whose rank entitled them to be presented to the monarch when they made their debut in the adult world.[19] After the wedding the trimmings could be removed or replaced with less significant flowers.

A painting by Frederick Daniel Hardy (1826–1911) called *The Wedding Dress* shows a dressmaker's workroom (pl.60), including a box of orange-blossom trimmings. The room is depicted as day breaks, shedding a golden light over a group of young girls who have been working all night to complete a wedding dress trimmed with orange-blossom. Although sewing machines, which were commercially viable by the 1850s, were used for the seams of clothes, most trimmings were laboriously applied by hand. The working conditions of dressmakers were a cause of public concern and a focus for social and political reformers throughout the nineteenth century. This painting highlights the long hours milliners had to work to complete commissions for demanding clients and, with one girl faint with exhaustion, the deleterious effects on their health.

BRIDESMAIDS

Bridesmaids added to the spectacle and charm of church weddings. It was customary for their families to pay for their clothes, but they expected to receive a gift from the bridegroom. Some women chose adult attendants. The opera singer Adelina Patti (1843–1919) was photographed with her husband Henri, Marquis de Caux (1825–99) and her four

60 *The Wedding Dress*, Frederick Daniel Hardy (1826–1911), oil on canvas, mid-1860s.

© Gallery Oldham UK / The Bridgeman Art Library

bridesmaids after her Roman Catholic wedding in Clapham, south London on 29 July 1868 (pl.61). The photograph seems to show the bridesmaids dressed in white but a newspaper report describes their wreaths, neck ribbons and sashes as blue, the colour of true love. Each wears a veil and carries a bouquet like the bride. The bride had arrived at the church with her veil enveloping her body but drew it back from her face for the photograph.[20]

Lady Audrey Townshend (1844–1926) was attended by eight bridesmaids at her wedding to Greville Howard (1836–80), second son of the 17th Earl of Suffolk, in 1873. The bridesmaids were picturesquely dressed in pale blue silk trimmed with blue gauze flounces and silk bows edged with dark red velvet, with matching velvet ties around their necks. All wore blue silk stockings and boots with rosettes. But while the five older girls were dressed in blue and red bonnets, the trio of younger bridesmaids, who were sisters, sported large-brimmed, high-crowned straw hats, lined with blue silk and caught up at one side with blue and red feathers.[21] Fashions in bridesmaids' outfits changed but it was common for the older and younger girls to form two distinct but colour-co-ordinated groups, with the latter dressed more quaintly. Apart from the most senior bridesmaid, whose role was to look after the bride's bouquet, fan and scent bottle during the service and act as a witness, the rest had little to do other than look charming. However the bridesmaids also represented the 'sisterhood' of unmarried women and girls whose companionship was so much a part of a young woman's life. Many women enjoyed rich relationships with their sisters and female friends and leaving them was a wrench. The inclusion of male attendants happens later. References to page boys start to appear in the mid-1880s and become more frequent from the 1890s.

The desire for the trappings of a fashionable wedding sometimes caused unwanted press attention. When the Quakers Mariana Louisa Rake (b.1847) and David Fry (b.1834) married in Bristol in 1867 with an entourage of bridesmaids, the Meeting House was crowded with guests whose carriages waited outside. The wedding inspired a poem in the satirical magazine *Punch* contrasting their worldliness with the sobriety of previous generations.[22] The verses attacked the bride's white silk train, pearl-edged veil and orange-blossom spray worn instead of the traditional deep-brimmed Quaker bonnet. The poem judged the bridesmaids '"Gainst Friends" rule'. The point of the satire was that even members of strict non-conformist sects like the Quakers were now being seduced into emulating society weddings. The wedding of Lucretia Anson Crouch (b.1842) and Benjamin Seebohm (b.1839), who married at the Friends Meeting House in Clevedon on 10 September 1874, was probably a quieter occasion. The groom was a widower with a young daughter and manager of the Luton branch of the family bank, Sharples, Tuke, Lucas and Seebohm.[23] Lucretia Crouch chose an ivory striped silk gauze outfit in the 'polonaise' style (pls 62–3), trimmed with satin bows and delicate cream machine-made lace. The polonaise, in which the bodice was extended to form an overskirt that could be gathered into a soft puff behind, resembled the eighteenth-century garment of the same name (pl.28). The volume of skirts had

61 Adelina Patti and Henri, Marquis de Caux, carte de visite, 1868. The photograph by Southwell Brothers shows four bridesmaids alongside the opera singer and her husband at their Roman Catholic wedding.
V&A: S.136:233–2007

62 Silk gauze wedding dress, British, 1874. The bodice and skirt were worn by the Quaker Lucretia Crouch for her marriage to Benjamin Seebohm in 1874.
V&A: T.68 to B–1962.
Given by Felicity Ashbee

63 'The Fashions', *The Englishwoman's Domestic Magazine*, c.1872. This fashion plate shows a bride in a similar dress. Like many in the magazine, the plate was first published in Paris.
V&A: E.2221–1888

64 Gold and pearl tiara by Castellani, Rome, 1860–69. Inspired by an Etruscan wreath from the 4th century BC, the tiara was given by the Earl of Crawford to his bride in 1869.

V&A: M.63–1921. Given by Emily, Dowager Countess of Crawford

65 Lace bridal veil (detail), Brussels, c.1890. Roxana Atwater Wentworth (1854–1935) wore this veil when she married American newspaper proprietor Clarence Winthrop Bowen (1852–1935) in 1892 in Chicago. According to their descendants it was exhibited at the Chicago World's Fair in 1893. Promoting excellence in design and manufacture, such exhibitions included a wide range of textiles.

V&A: T.366–1970

moved to the back by the mid-1860s, and in the 1870s it was contained with elaborate drapery. The bride's dress was fashionable but unexceptional, reflecting a deliberate desire, shared by many Quakers, to appear well-dressed but unobtrusive.

VEILS AND TIARAS

Jewellery was as important to the appearance of aristocratic and upper-class brides in the nineteenth century as it had been for most of the previous century. It was traditional for the bride's father and the bridegroom to give the bride jewellery to wear on her wedding day, and from the late 1860s hair ornaments such as tiaras, aigrettes and pins which could be worn with the veil were popular. The jewels were worn afterwards for formal evening occasions and though many were new in the nineteenth century they became family heirlooms and were worn by subsequent generations. In 1869 James Lord Lindsay, later 26th Earl of Crawford (1847–1913), gave his bride Emily Bootle Wilbraham (1848–1934) a pearl and gold tiara made by the prestigious Roman firm Castellani (pl.64). The design in the form of a myrtle wreath reflects the vogue for jewellery based on archaeological models, and was inspired by an Etruscan wreath from the fourth century BC. Myrtle was emblematic of love.

When Henry Fitzalan-Howard, 15th Duke of Norfolk (1847–1917), married Lady Flora Abney-Hastings (1854–87) on 21 November 1877 at the Brompton Oratory, a fashionable Roman Catholic church in London's Knightsbridge, the bride dazzled with diamonds. They included a coronet of nine diamond stars given by her father, a diamond necklace presented by the groom from which hung a diamond pendant given by her future mother-in-law, and diamond earrings presented by her brother. The bride wore another diamond necklace and several diamond bracelets given by family tenants. These jewels expressed the wealth and status of the two families united by the marriage. The bride's *point de gaze* lace veil had won a prize at the Fourth Annual International Exhibition held in London in 1874.[24] The nineteenth-century international exhibitions were held in cities across the globe and played an important role in encouraging manufacturers to improve the design and manufacture of their products. They also offered the public an opportunity to see good design and fine workmanship, potentially raising standards of public taste (pls 65–6).

In the second half of the nineteenth century there was a revival of interest in lace and a set of lace was a desirable acquisition for a bride. According to Charlotte Treadwin, author of *Antique Point and Honiton Lace* (c.1874), the set should include a veil, a deep flounce suitable for a skirt with a matching narrow trimming, lappets for evening wear, a pocket handkerchief and a fan leaf (pl.67).[25] Treadwin was a very skilled lacemaker with a shop in Exeter in Devon. She successfully exhibited her lace at the Great Exhibition in London in 1851 and the Exposition Universelle in Paris in 1867. London had a number of specialist lace dealers who sold modern and antique lace, which was particularly prized at this period.

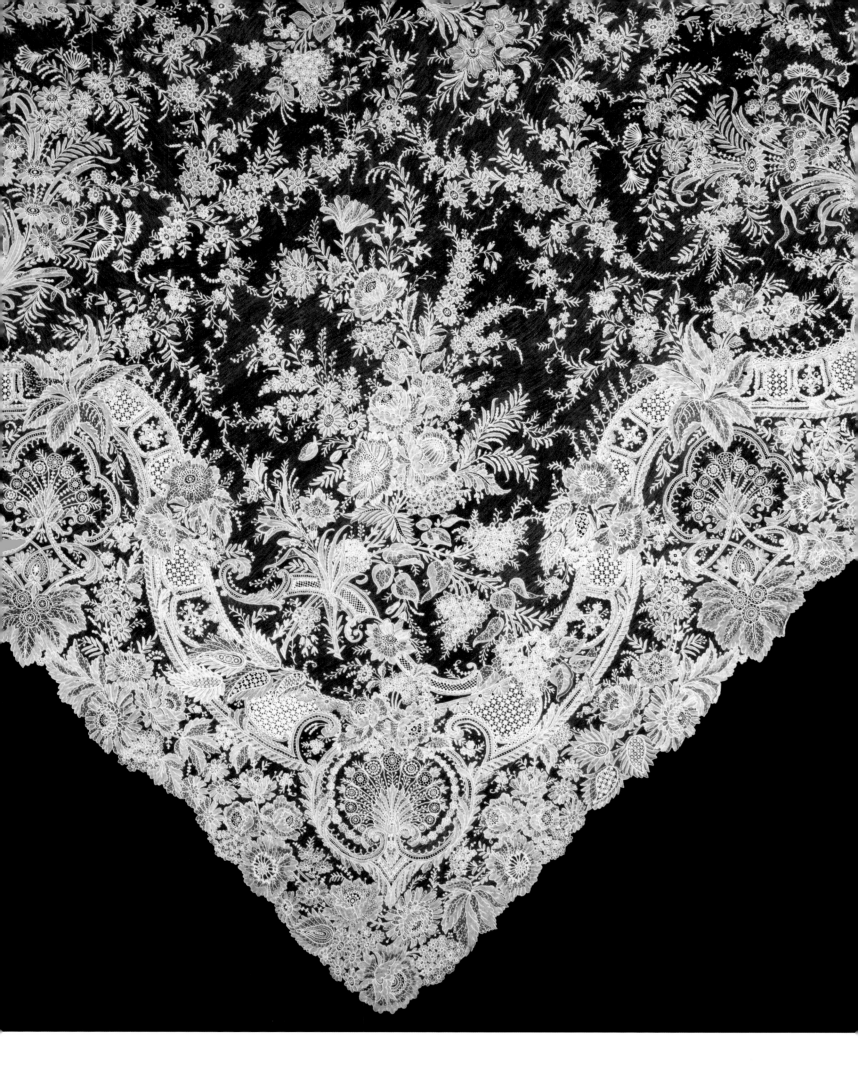

66 Lace bridal veil (details)
V&A: T.366–1970

67 Silk lace fan leaf
made by Georges Robert, Courseulles-sur-Mer, Normandy, 1899. American heiress Mary Ethel Burns (d.1961) ordered this fan leaf from Worth of Paris as part of her trousseau. She married Lewis (later 1st Viscount) Harcourt (1863–1922) on 1 July 1899. She purchased a matching handkerchief and dress flounce.

V&A: T.30–1965. Given from the collection of Mary, Viscountess Harcourt CBE

NEW FASHIONS

By the mid-1870s, the skirts of bridal dresses often extended into trains like formal day and evening wear but the introduction of separate trains, attached at the shoulders or waist, was an innovation. In 1881 they were recommended for brides who had chosen a more practical 'short' (untrained) dress.[26] Trains added dignity to the ensemble and depending on their length and decoration created a dramatic spectacle as the bride processed to the chancel steps. When a bride was presented at court following her wedding, it was customary for her to wear her wedding dress (adapted for evening wear by removing the sleeves and lowering the neckline) with a special court train. The train was usually made of a richer fabric than the dress, such as velvet, and the Lord Chancellor's Office prescribed its dimensions and methods of attachment. A bride could wear the same train for her wedding and presentation provided it accorded with court etiquette.

Clara Mathews (b. about 1855) ordered her wedding dress (pl.69) with a separate velvet train from the House of Worth in Paris when she became engaged to Colonel Hugh Stafford (b. about 1835). She was an illegitimate daughter of Isaac Merritt Singer, the American founder of the Singer Sewing Machine Company. Charles Frederick Worth (1825–95) was Paris's leading dressmaker. Born and apprenticed in England, he was celebrated for confident designs that translated into immaculately cut garments, and the flair with which he selected and handled fabric. He was also a gifted publicist and self-styled artist. He had an international clientele and his extremely costly designs were particularly admired by wealthy North Americans like Clara Mathews.

The couple married at the society church of St George's Hanover Square in London on 19 February 1880. The bride's ivory silk satin outfit has a tailored bodice-jacket with a lobed basque edged with a fringe of pearl beads. Though probably trimmed with a corsage of orange-blossoms (pl.68), the jacket's austere simplicity contrasts with the skirt which is lavishly decorated with opaque and pearlized beads worked into fringes and tassels, and panels of net embroidered with feathery leaves whose stems are accentuated with beads. More beads have been used to create buds and flowers, and to decorate three-dimensional fabric bell-flowers. The pendant pearls would have rippled and shimmered with the movements of the bride, infusing the dress with a subtle sensuality. Pearls were a newly fashionable trimming for wedding gowns. Charles Gask & Company of Oxford Street exhibited a white satin bridal gown whose bodice was 'honeycombed' with pearl beads at the Grand Wedding Exhibition held in December 1881 at London's Royal Aquarium. This exhibition, which was probably the first 'bridal fair' to be held in Britain, included stands displaying the goods and services offered by dressmakers, jewellers, caterers, florists, stationers, photographers and furniture makers.[27]

68 'Toilette de Mariée',
La Mode Artistique, Paris,
August 1880. Gustave Janet's
lithograph shows a bride
wearing a corsage of
orange-blossom pinned to
her bodice.
V&A: E.158–1951

As the nineteenth century drew to a close, styles inspired by historical costume, which contemporary writers described as 'picturesque', became increasingly fashionable. The wedding dress of Cara Leland Rogers (1868–1939), purchased from Stern Brothers of New York in 1890, reflects this trend and the new fashion for plainer, narrow skirts paired with lavishly decorated bodices (pl.70). The dress, which is a copy of a Paquin, Lalanne et Cie model, has a rigidly boned bodice with a basque and trained skirt of cream corded silk overlaid with silk crêpe. The bodice's sleeves increase in size towards the sleeve head and puff out above it alongside wired net wings that mark and frame the shoulder line. The wings, bodice and edges of the basque are appliquéd with pale apricot-coloured velvet embellished with faux

pearls and diamanté, metal and glass beads which together create a scrolling pattern of stylized leaves, fruits and flowers. The flower resembles a lily, symbolizing purity, and the fruit a pomegranate, emblematic of fertility. Tragically, Cara's husband Bradford Ferris Duff (*c*.1867–91), a fellow American whom she married on 17 November 1890 in New York, died within a year of their marriage.[28]

The fashion for picturesque styles continued into the new century. They were a feature of high fashion, but also appealed to women who wished to dress artistically. While a few women rejected mainstream fashion altogether, others chose to express their individuality in a more moderate way, wearing fashionable garments but discreetly customizing them to express their sense of style.

**69 Embroidered silk
wedding dress** (bodice and
skirt) by Charles Frederick
Worth, Paris, 1880. The dress
is an early example of the
use of pearl beads on bridal
wear.
V&A: T.62&A–1976.
Given by Mrs G.T. Morton

70 Wedding dress (front and back) by Stern Brothers, New York, 1890, based on a Paris model created by Paquin, Lalanne et Cie. At the end of the nineteenth century there was a vogue for 'picturesque' styles inspired by historical dress. Jewelled 'wings' at the sleeve head had been a feature of women's dress in the latter part of the sixteenth century.
V&A: T.276&A–1972. Given by Major and Mrs Broughton

71 Wedding corset (front and back), silk satin and whalebone trimmed with machine lace and silk chiffon, British, 1905. This luxury corset was custom-made for a bride. It was designed to create the fashionable S-bend silhouette but its fabric and construction, which balance function with decoration, would have provided only light control over the lower abdomen.

V&A: T.90-1928.
Given by Mrs G.E. Dixon

Dressing artistically was a recognized strand in British fashion. It had been promoted by the Aesthetic Movement which flourished in the 1870s and 1880s and was encouraged by the Arts and Crafts Movement, which upheld the tradition of hand-production and argued that decoration should relate to an object's form and function. When Alice Grosvenor (1880–1948) wanted a dress for her marriage to Ivor Churchill Guest (1873–1939) on 10 February 1902, she went to the London court dressmaker Sarah Fullerton Monteith Young (b. about 1844), who was known for dressing clients who wanted their clothes to reflect their artistic sensibility.[29] The cut of the dress follows the fashionable silhouette which had evolved from the hour-glass profile favoured in the Victorian period to a more S-shaped form. This was

achieved using corsetry (pl.71) to push the stomach and pelvis in, hips back and bosom forward, creating the appearance of a low full bust, elongated waist and arched back (pl.72). The dress's materials are also conventional but its decoration, designed by the bride, is unique. Bands of embroidered, hand-painted blue arabesques framing clusters of flowers are appliquéd to the skirt (pl.73) while chains of smaller, simpler motifs decorate the bodice. The bride completed her outfit with an antique lace veil lent by her mother, which she wore over a tiara of artificial orange-blossom. Her only jewels were diamond shoe buckles given to her by the groom and she carried a sheaf of arum lilies.[30]

Many women who wished to dress artistically without appearing outlandish patronized Liberty's in London's Regent Street. Arthur Lasenby Liberty (1843–1917), who opened his first shop in 1875, was at the heart of the nineteenth-century artistic movements which aimed to improve British design and public taste. In 1884 he introduced a costume department, offering historically inspired clothes made from Liberty fabrics under the guidance of the designer and architect Edward William Godwin (1833–86). By the twentieth century Liberty's advertised picturesque costumes of the past 'combining distinction and refinement and NEVER OUT OF FASHION', alongside costumes of the present 'reproduced from the latest Parisienne fashion supplied by Liberty & Co. staff in Paris'. Their 1907 bridal catalogue drew on Puritan, Restoration and Empire styles of dress adapted for the bride, adult and child bridesmaid and page.[31] A white satin medieval-style wedding dress from Liberty's of around 1907–8 has a collar and pendant girdle with dog roses, leaves and interlacing stems embroidered in white satin stitch and embellished with faux pearls (pl.74). The same motifs are used to create a border pattern for the dress's matching three and a half metre train. The design is reminiscent of the embroideries designed at the Glasgow School of Art, whose innovative embroidery department was established by artist Jessie Newbery (1864–1948) in 1894.

Girls wishing to join the workrooms of London's exclusive dressmakers and department stores, which specialized in hand-crafted, made-to-measure clothes for wealthy clients, could apply to work as 'learners' in an informal apprenticeship. However many houses relied on skilled workers from the Continent, supplemented at busy periods by low-paid, locally sourced casual labour. These hiring practices led to economic hardship in the industry and a lack of training opportunities that eventually caused a shortage of skills. To remedy this, girls' needle-trade schools were set up at the Borough Polytechnic in 1904 and the Shoreditch Technical Institute in 1906 (pl.75). During the two-year full-time course the students, who started between the ages of 12 and 14, spent two thirds of their time learning the skills of their chosen trade. The school committees, which helped set the curriculum, included representatives

building was well filled with the numerous friends of both families, among whom were the Duke of Westminster, the Marquis of Londonderry, Lord and Lady Wimborne, Lady Ebury, the Marquis and Marchioness Camden, Viscount Duncannon, the Countess of Ancaster, Countess Deym and Countess Isabella Deym, Lord Chesham, the Countess of Lichfield and Lady Bertha Anson, the Hon. Mrs Norman Grosvenor, Lady Rodney, the Earl and Countess of Scarbrough, Lady Gerard, the Countess of Aberdeen and Lady Marjorie Gordon, &c. Mr Claude Lowther, M.P., acted as best man to the bridegroom. The bride was accompanied to the chancel by her father, who gave her away, and was followed by no fewer than fourteen bridesmaids. As the procession passed up the nave, preceded by the boy choristers, "Blessed City, Heavenly Salem," was sung. The Bishop of London performed the ceremony, and the Rev. Prebendary Storrs, M.A., vicar of the parish, and the Rev. C. M. O. Parkinson, M.A., Vicar of Rickmansworth, took part in the service. The Bishop gave an eloquent address after "O, perfect Love," had been sung, and before the Benediction, "Holy, Holy, Holy! Lord God Almighty!" was given. The anthem was Spohr's "Children, pray this love to cherish," sung while the register was being signed. The bride wore a trained gown of white lisse, exquisitely embroidered with hand-painted lisse and silver in a wreath design of her own, the whole being mounted over crystalline silk. The over dress was bordered with tiny frills of chiffon edged with dull silver, and the bodice, which was draped with lisse and embroidery bolero fashion, was finished with a collar of real lace, while the rucked sleeves, fastened with diamond buttons, were held in round the arm with a band

from court dressmakers and stores like Liberty's and Selfridge's to ensure that students learned the right skills to find a job.[32]

Towards the end of the first decade of the twentieth century, the S-bend gave way to a straight, slim, high-waisted silhouette which was described as the Directoire style. The dress Clementine Hosier (1885–1977) wore when she wed the politician Winston Churchill (1874–1965) on 12 September 1908 was cut in this style. It was inspired by Juliet's robe in an 1884 painting by Frank Dicksee (1853–1928) that recreated the balcony scene in William Shakespeare's play *Romeo and Juliet*. In the painting Juliet wears a plain, round-necked, white chemise dress with full sleeves, whose soft drapery reveals the shape of her legs as it falls in a pool of fabric on the floor. The bride's white satin gown was trimmed at the neck with antique *point de Venise* lace and it had short sleeves with turned-back lace cuffs and a long train.[33] However descriptions of the bride's dress and plain tulle veil, held in place with a diadem of fresh orange-blossom, praise their simplicity. Her dress was made by Madame Marte of Conduit Street. While the *Daily Express* praised the bride's taste for 'sumptuous simplicity', the *Tailor and Cutter* described Churchill's outfit as 'one of the greatest

72 'Hon. Alice Grosvenor's Wedding Gown', *The Queen*, 15 February 1902. The gown reflects the new S-bend silhouette which was achieved through corsetry.
V&A: National Art Library

73 Embroidery from a silk wedding dress by Sarah Fullerton Monteith Young, London, 1902. In keeping with artistic fashion, the bride Alice Grosvenor designed the embroidery herself.
V&A: T.215B–1976.
Gift of Viscount Wimborne

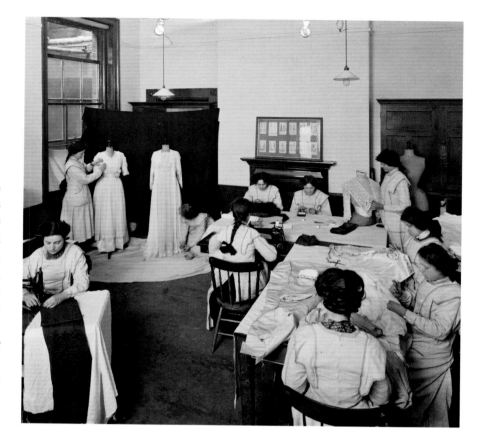

failures as a wedding garment we have ever seen, giving the wearer a sort of glorified coachman appearance'.[34] In the *Tailor and Cutter*'s eyes, the groom's mistake was probably to have chosen a frock coat rather than a morning coat, which was the more usual formal morning wear for young gentlemen, and his preference for wearing it buttoned up rather than open (pl.76). However Churchill had a typically British approach to clothing and followed his own sartorial tastes while keeping within the bounds of etiquette.

The period framed by Queen Victoria's wedding in 1840 and the outbreak of the First World War in 1914 was the heyday of the white wedding dress. The increasing scale of weddings and the publicity given to them encouraged businesses to develop wedding-specific services, which they promoted with increasingly sophisticated forms of advertising targeting the middle and upper classes. Classified advertisements, catalogues, exhibitions and editorial were all used to promote wedding-related products. White became so conventional for bridal wear for the upper classes that descriptions of fashionable wedding dresses sometimes omitted their colour.[35] However towards the end of the period, fashionable brides and those with a highly developed personal

style, like Alice Grosvenor, tired of the orthodox ensemble of white wedding dress, orange-blossom wreath and lace veil. Embroidery worked in silk and faux pearl, gold, silver and bronze beads started to replace swags of orange-blossom from the 1880s, and touches of colours other than white or cream are occasionally found on wedding dresses. In the years before the First World War, wedding dresses with short and elbow-length sleeves became fashionable, heralding a link between evening fashions and bridal wear that was developed in the succeeding decades.

75 Shoreditch Technical Institute, c.1911. The pupils are learning dressmaking techniques.

© London Metropolitan Archive

76 Winston Churchill on his wedding day, 1908. The photograph shows the politician arriving at the doors of St Margaret's Church, Westminster for his marriage to Clementine Hosier.

Private collection / Stapleton Collection / The Bridgeman Art Library

Too old for white

On 8 June 1899 **Harriett Joyce** (b.1863) married
Percy Raven Sams (b.1870) at St Andrew's Church,
Earlsfield, Middlesex.[1] She wore a crisply tailored
purple silk grosgrain bodice and skirt that she had
made herself (pl.78). Purple was associated with
bereavement, but it was also a practical colour
choice for a silk dress intended to be worn again
for best after the ceremony. Harriett chose a
coloured dress because, aged thirty-five, she
considered herself too old a bride to wear white.
Nonetheless she incorporated cream satin
and lace into the bodice and wore wax orange-
blossom on her hat.[2]

In spite of the many dressmakers catering to
all social levels in the nineteenth century and the
increasing availability of ready-made garments
from the 1860s onwards, many women continued
making their own clothes. The availability of
sewing machines, commercially printed dress
patterns and affordable machine-woven silks
and trimmings enabled skilled needlewomen to
produce sophisticated gowns such as this one.

When Harriett married Percy Sams, who
worked for the Water Board in London, she left
her post as a lady's maid to Mrs Frances Boevey.
She had been in service from a young age,
following one of the principal options for young
working-class girls seeking to make their living in
the late nineteenth century. Harriett started out as
a nursemaid in Essex, but worked her way up to a
position of greater responsibility as a lady's maid.
The Boevey family lived on West Cromwell Road
in West Kensington, a very respectable neighbour-
hood. Mr Boevey was a solicitor, and his
neighbours included two barristers and a
retired colonel.[3]

As a lady's maid, Harriett would have looked
after her employer's wardrobe. Good sewing skills
were essential, and the workmanship in her wedding dress is exceptionally fine. The dress is lined
throughout with cotton and lightweight canvas,
and finished to a very high standard (pl.77). Soon
after the wedding, Harriett altered the skirt by
removing two side gores to update the dress and
create a more fashionable narrower silhouette.

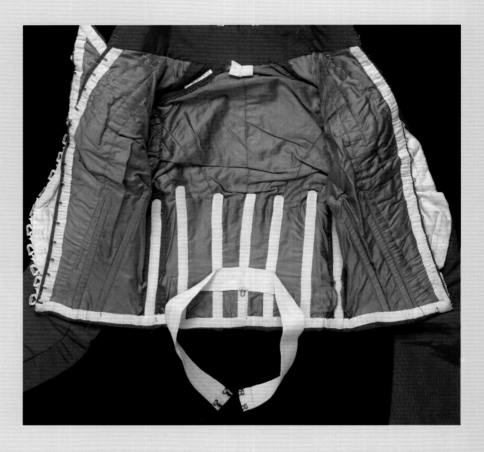

She also added purple silk braid to the front of the
skirt, perhaps so it could be worn separately with
a blouse. The alterations are so neatly done as to
be indiscernible. Harriett kept the surplus fabric
and stored it alongside the dress. Following the
birth of her daughter Dorothy in 1900, it is possible
that the dress no longer fitted, so Harriett stored it
away. Its survival in near-pristine condition testi-
fies to her dressmaking skills, her choice of
good-quality fabrics and the care she took of her
clothes. It also shows the type of dress that would
have been chosen as a practical wedding option by
a woman of her class.

When Harriett's granddaughter donated the
dress to the V&A in 1982, she recalled that her
grandmother was a tiny, trimly dressed, brisk
woman with a great sense of economy, who had
bought her marital home in Wandsworth with
her savings.

Daniel Milford-Cottam

**77 Silk grosgrain wedding
dress** (detail) showing the
inside of the boned bodice
and its waistband. The bride
was a skilful dressmaker
who made her own wedding
dress.
V&A: T.309&A–1982.
Given by Mrs Muriel Baker

**78 Silk grosgrain wedding
dress** trimmed with satin
and lace, British, 1899.
V&A: T.309&A–1982.
Given by Mrs Muriel Baker

TOWARDS
THE MODERN
1914–45

nlike nineteenth-century bridal wear worn for church weddings, the fabric, cut, construction and decoration of fashionable wedding dresses in the interwar period followed evening styles rather than daywear. Wedding dresses in shades of white and cream remained popular, but there were alternatives to these colours.

The shift towards evening wear was gradual. It started in the Edwardian period and became more pronounced after the First World War, as daywear became more practical, informal and androgynous. In the 1920s metallic lamés and lace, pale gold and shell pink fabrics were fashionable for bridal and evening wear, giving wedding dresses added glamour. The classic white satin wedding dress returned to favour in the uncertain years of the Depression in the early 1930s, but in the second half of the decade pastel colours were an alternative to white. In 1934 the hours regulating when marriages could take place in church were extended from 3pm until 6pm and the opportunity to move on from the wedding to an evening reception may have encouraged a more open-minded approach to what colour a wedding dress should be. Brides were guided in their choice by morality, religious sentiment, personal taste, budget and the strength of their engagement with fashion.

Film became an important influence on wedding styles. The introduction of commercially viable films in the mid-1890s and of picture houses in the early twentieth century was one of the most important technological developments in the first half of the twentieth century. Film enabled people to see with astonishing immediacy fashionable events that they had only read about or seen in still images in the past. It introduced a new way of exchanging information, a medium for entertainment and an alternative to photography for recording celebrity and newsworthy events such as weddings.

WEDDINGS IN THE FIRST WORLD WAR

A 1914 wedding dress (pl.79) is a good example of the influence of evening wear on bridal fashions at the start of the First World War (1914–18). Phyllis Blaiberg (b.1886) married Bertie Mayer Stone at the Bayswater Synagogue near London's Hyde Park on 9 September, a month after the outbreak of the war. She chose a tunic-shaped, ankle-length dress with a V-shaped back and neckline and short sleeves. Its slightly raised waistline is marked by a broad white

79 Beaded wedding dress
by Aida Woolf, London, 1914. Woolf's shop at 283 Oxford Street was above the ABC teashop. Her salon was on the first floor, the family living quarters on the second and the workrooms in the attics.
V&A: T.856&A–1974.
Gift of Mrs B. Rackow

80 Silk and leather 'tango' shoes bought from Peter Robinson of London, 1914.
V&A: T.856B, C–1974.
Gift of Mrs B. Rackow

**81 Beaded wedding
dress** (details) showing
the satin panel at the
back and the train.
V&A: T.856&A–1974.
Gift of Mrs B. Rackow

satin sash which extends to the hips and a satin panel hanging down the skirt back (pl.81). The dress is made from ivory satin, overlaid with machine-made lace with a dense floral pattern embellished with diamanté, and finished with a tulle overdress edged with diamanté. It has a matching lace train (pl.81), which is lined with pink tulle and decorated with a white tulle bow and frill.

The dress's materials, construction, scalloped hemline and the bow, or true lover's knot, on the train were all the height of fashion. Over time the tulle has become grey and matted and it is now difficult to appreciate how soft and pretty it would have looked. The new shorter hemlines revealed the shoes, leading to the introduction of more decorative styles of footwear. The bride chose a pair of silver and white silk 'tango' shoes which fasten with silver laces threaded through eyelets designed with tiny, metal bows set with diamantés (pl.80). The tango had been introduced from Argentina to Europe and North America and by 1913 the dance had become a craze.

Phyllis Blaiberg ordered her wedding dress from Aida Woolf (1886–1967) who had a shop in Oxford Street. As today, this was the busiest shopping street in the West End of London. Its north side was lined with huge department stores such as Selfridges, (which had opened in 1909) and Peter Robinson, where Phyllis purchased her shoes. These new stores attracted thousands of shoppers from London's expanding suburbs. Aida Woolf had recently moved to Oxford Street from premises in the south London suburb of Brixton. She was born Ada Woolf in Mile End in the East End of London, where the ready-made dress and tailoring trades were located, and worked her way up from a dressmaking apprenticeship in Hackney to owning her own couture house in the West End. Three sisters, described in the 1911 census as assistant dressmakers and a milliner, worked with her.[1] Woolf was Jewish and many of her clients came from London's upper-middle-class Jewish community. Her success enabled her to continue to upgrade her retail address and by 1938 she had premises at 20 Grosvenor Street in Mayfair, alongside the couturier Edward Molyneux's London fashion house. The V&A has another Aida Woolf design made for Flora Diamond, who married Phillip Jacobs at the Bayswater Synagogue in 1923 (pl.82). The wedding dress is made from silver lamé with a beaded silver lace overskirt and its train is decorated with appliquéd pink silk leaves.[2]

During the First World War many women married in smart daywear, but some managed to have a white wedding. Bridegrooms serving in the armed forces typically married in uniform. When the American singer and costume designer Grace Crawford (1889–1977) married the British artist and designer Claud Lovat Fraser (1890–1921) on 6 February 1917 in London, she wore a dress designed by her husband-to-be. He had been invalided out of the army suffering from shell shock and exposure to gas, but had found work designing visual propaganda. The bride's dress, made at home by a maid, consisted of a cloth of gold tunic and long skirt of cream-coloured velvet. Her four bridesmaids were dressed in scarlet and gold brocade tunics over cream chiffon skirts. Although Grace Crawford rejected a conventional white dress, she wore her mother's cream net wedding veil held in place by a wreath of real myrtle leaves and small gold-tissue oranges. Her bouquet of sulphur-yellow carnations and stiff gilded leaves was tied with Lovat's regimental colours.[3] Some more sophisticated brides were wearing dresses made of metallic fabrics and velvet from around 1912, but the materials became more fashionable after the war.

Both world wars were catalysts for political and social change. During the First World War more than three quarters of a million servicemen from the British Isles were killed and many of the survivors were disabled, leaving families with no male earner and a surplus of unmarried women. Women played an important role in the war on the home front and, from 1916, in the armed forces. The contribution of women to the war effort and their right to full employment were acknowledged after the war by sweeping political reforms which integrated women into public life and expanded the range of careers open to them. In 1918 women over the age of thirty were granted the legal right to vote and stand for Parliament and in 1928 these rights were extended to all women over the age of twenty-one. In 1919 the

82 Flora Diamond and Phillip Jacobs on their wedding day, London, June 1923. Aida Woolf made the bride's striking silver lamé dress, which has a beaded silver lace overskirt and a train decorated with appliquéd pink silk leaves.

Photograph by Thomas Fall Studio. V&A: Furniture, Textiles and Fashion Archive

Sex Disqualification (Removal) Act opened up universities, the law, the civil service and professions organized by incorporated societies, such as accountancy, to single and married women.

Fashions for daywear in the 1920s reflected the emancipation of women and their more active lives. Clothes were neat, practical and loose-fitting. Evening styles by contrast were glamorous and revealing, and inspired by an eclectic range of sources that included medieval dress and quasi-oriental styles. Lamé, lace, tulle and velvet were popular fabrics and beading a favoured form of decoration. They were designed for the hedonistic lifestyle of the generation who had come of age during the war and who found relief from the years of grief and destruction in a frenetic round of night clubs, impromptu parties and casual invitations. Although the young and rich rejected the formal, planned social life of their elders, they conformed to the traditional social rites of passage and marriage remained the goal of most women.

Paris continued to dominate the international market in women's fashion and in 1919 the talented and ambitious young Anglo-Irish couturier Edward Molyneux (1891–1974) opened his house in Paris. Molyneux had trained with the celebrated Lucile

(Lady Duff-Gordon, 1862–1935) at her houses in London, Paris and New York. However in the 1920s and 1930s Britain benefited from the presence of a group of creative young designers who established couture houses in London, run on similar lines to Paris but on a smaller scale, with French and British staff. They included Norman Hartnell (1901–79), who launched his label in 1923 and soon won an international reputation, and the South African-born Victor Stiebel (1907–76), who opened a house in Bruton Street, off Bond Street, near Hartnell's house in 1932. Both men excelled at romantic evening wear and wedding dresses that flattered the wearer and were appropriate for the occasion and its location.

WEDDING FASHIONS ON FILM

The first British royal wedding after the war was the marriage of Princess Patricia of Connaught (1886–1974) to Commander Alexander Ramsay (1881–1972). The princess was a much-loved public figure and her popularity increased following her decision to voluntarily relinquish her royal title to become nearer in rank to her husband and be known simply as Lady Patricia. Aspects of the wedding, which took place on 27 February 1919, were filmed by Pathé Frères to be distributed as newsreels.[4] The crowd scenes shown in the short film are impressive but viewers only got a tantalizing glimpse of the bride wearing a lamé wrap with a deep white fur collar which hid her brocaded cream panné velvet dress and lily-embroidered cloth of silver train. As the royal procession neared Westminster Abbey, the crowd was swelled by thousands of young female office workers cheering for 'Princess Pat'. The London correspondent of the *Manchester Guardian* emphasized the women's romantic engagement with the princess and her story: 'no play about a triumphant heroine and no last chapter of a novel had ever thrilled them like this vision of a royal romance come true. Certainly no imagined heroine could have looked more beautiful than the pale Princess.'[5]

The first fully publicized royal wedding was the marriage of Princess Mary (1897–1965), daughter of George V and Queen Mary, to Viscount Lascelles (1882–1947) on 28 February 1922. The films of the preparations and wedding day demonstrate more

83 **'Bridal Veils for Wedding Belles'**, *Eve's Film Review*, *c*.1923. The film showed wedding styles inspired by the bridal veil and headdress worn by Elizabeth Bowes-Lyon when she married Albert, Duke of York (later George VI).
© British Pathé

sophisticated cinematic techniques and a greater appreciation of what audiences wanted to see. The bride was filmed on her way to and from Westminster Abbey, placing a bouquet on the cenotaph and, in a now traditional scene, waving to the crowds from the balcony of Buckingham Palace. Her dress, like Princess Patricia's, was supplied by Reville & Rossiter, one of London's leading court dressmakers. It was made of silk gauze embroidered with pearl and crystal beads mounted over silver lamé, with a train of silver and ivory satin embroidered in silver with the emblems of the Empire. Her silver wreath was entwined with orange-blossom.[6] Wearing fabric incorporating silver was traditional for royal brides but it was also fashionable in the 1920s. The wedding was filmed by at least four competing cinematograph firms, including Gaumont and Pathé, who distributed the film by train and aeroplane to picture houses across the country on the day of the wedding. When the films arrived in New York on 9 March, messengers from news and film agencies swarmed aboard the ship in a mad scramble to get the first pictures. Cheered on by passengers, they did their best to elude the customs officials in scenes of slapstick comedy.[7] The money invested in distributing the newsreels attests to the continuing interest in royal weddings, which undoubtedly fuelled bridal dreams of becoming a princess for a day.

The next royal wedding took place on 26 April 1923 at Westminster Abbey, and united Lady Elizabeth Bowes-Lyon (1900–2002) and Albert, Duke of York (later George VI) (1895–1952), future parents of the present queen. The bride wore a medieval-inspired, loose-fitting dress of ivory chiffon moiré with a square neckline and short sleeves made by Lon-

84 **Sketch of a wedding dress** by Worth, pencil, ink and body colour, London, *c*.1922.
V&A: E.22921–1957.
Given by the House of Worth

85 **'Paris Outvied'**, *Pathé Gazette*, 1923. This still from a newsreel shows Molyneux models in a London fashion show staged at the Women's Exhibition at Olympia.
© British Pathé

don's Madame Handley-Seymour. The front of the bodice was appliquéd with horizontal bands of silver lamé, embellished with gold embroidery and pearl and paste beads. A single vertical band decorated the front of the trained skirt. A separate tulle and lace train was attached to her shoulders. Her Flanders lace veil, lent to her by Queen Mary, was held in place with a circlet of myrtle which was decorated at the sides with knots of white roses and heather, reflecting her Scottish ancestry.[8] The arrangement of her veil and wreath inspired a film for Pathé's cinemagazine, *Eve's Film Review*, which was launched in April 1921 as part of the supporting programme in Pathé's cinemas. *Bridal Veils for Wedding Belles* shows close-ups of three similar headdresses created by 'Emile' (pl.83). The models smile, simper or look demure, creating an atmosphere of coy intimacy while the audience can see the headdresses in the round and potentially identify with a particular model and style.[9] Headdresses were worn low over the brow and veils over or away from the face throughout the 1920s. A sketch of a bridal dress designed by Worth from about 1922 evokes the misty aura created around the bride when the veil enveloped the body (pl.84). It also highlights the new interest in the neck and shoulders, the lower waistline and full skirt that were fashionable in the early 1920s.

Film was the perfect medium for conveying the glamour and atmosphere of the fashion show. When Edward Molyneux displayed his latest models at the Women's Exhibition at Olympia in 1923, the event was filmed by Pathé.[10] The short newsreel features models dressed as a bride, bridesmaids and two flower girls (pl.85). At the end of the show the designer joined the bride, who was dressed in a gold lamé sheath dress accessorized with an Egyptian-style headdress and long string of pearls. She carried a sheaf of lilies, which had become the wedding flower of choice. Molyneux, whose clients included the actresses Gladys Cooper and Gertrude Lawrence, was already known for designing immaculately made clothes of luxurious, refined elegance. His appearance at the end of the show was a compliment to the audience, but also demonstrates an increasing awareness of the importance of public relations.

86 Bride, *c.*1926.
The new silhouette for women was flat-chested, slim-hipped and athletic.
Photograph by Peter North. V&A: Furniture, Textiles and Fashion Archive

87 Silk velvet wedding dress embroidered with pearls, with replica lace chemisette, British, 1927. Medieval styles remained popular throughout the 1920s.
V&A: T.126–2009. Given by Oriel and Alicia Robinson, direct descendants of Maud Cecil

1920S BRIDES

During the 1920s the hemlines of wedding dresses gradually shortened and by 1926 some were knee-length. The fashionable silhouette was flat-chested, slim-hipped and athletic, and the bride's head appeared small and neat. A studio photograph probably of the mid-1920s by Peter North shows an unknown bride wearing a fashionable slim-fitting, long-sleeved dress with a scalloped hem (pl.86). Apart from the trail of blossom attached to her head-dress, the most striking feature of her outfit is the transparent train which merges with her tulle veil to create a shimmering haze of light around her. An alternative was a train with a transparent 'window' from the shoulders, which enabled the congregation to appreciate the back of the bride's dress.[11] By the end of the 1920s it was customary for brides who wore their veil over their faces during the service to throw it back for the bridal procession at the end of the ceremony.[12]

For brides who preferred something less sophisticated, medieval styles remained popular. Maud Cecil's (1904–81) dress for her wedding to Richard Greville Acton Steel (1904–81) in 1927 reflects and reinterprets this fashion (pl.87). The full-length dress, which has a dropped waist and long sleeves extending to the knuckles, was made from pale gold 'ring' velvet. This type of velvet is very supple and has a high sheen. The skirt is embroidered with pearl beads in an unusual swirling pattern of exotic flowers and foliage merging the oriental with the medieval. The bride had studied art at the Slade School and her keen sense of form and colour are evident in her dress. Her father, Sir Evelyn Cecil, was a Member of Parliament and in the days leading up to her wedding on 17 November the *Daily Mirror* drip-fed the public with titbits of gossip about her fashion choices.[13] On the 12th readers were told: 'I hear that Miss Cecil has chosen the now popular scheme of shaded colours for her bridesmaids'(pl.89); two days later she and another society bride were commended for selecting ring velvet, 'the most popular material of the season'; and on the 18th readers were rewarded with a photograph of the bride and groom (pl.88). The pre-publicity given to weddings led to large,

88 Maud Cecil and Richard Steel, 1927. The bride wore her dress with a tulle veil and court train.

Private collection

89 Maud Cecil's bridesmaids, London, 1927. The bride's adult attendants wore paired dresses in a series of autumnal shades.

Private collection

predominantly female crowds gathering outside the church to see the bride and her dress.

In 1928 Marshall & Snelgrove, one of Oxford Street's most prestigious department stores, published a brochure advertising their services for brides-to-be.[14] Taking its inspiration from Mary Martha Sherwood's moral tales for children, *The History of the Fairchild Family* (in three volumes: 1818, 1842, 1847), it transports Lucy Fairchild and her mother from 1818 to 1928 and tells the story of their experiences choosing Lucy's trousseau at Marshall & Snelgrove.

The narrative charms through its device of time-travel. Mrs Fairchild's initial consternation when confronted with the skimpiness of contemporary styles leads to a growing confidence in the saleswoman, impressing upon readers that they too can trust the store to dress them fashionably and appropriately for every social occasion. The saleswoman is also adept at discreetly diffusing potential conflict between mother and daughter. The story climaxes with the appearance of a mannequin in a wedding dress so perfect that Lucy faints. The dress's colour, fitted bodice, long sleeves and dropped waistline have similarities with Maud Cecil's gown. Described as 'Moyen-age' (medieval), it is made of parchment and gold brocade, with its waist embroidered to simulate a girdle (pl.91). The Madonna lilies held aloft

by the mannequin are artificial, 'made of gold to tone with the gown'. Weddings were an important market for department stores and as this catalogue makes clear their aim was to provide the bride's trousseau as well as her wedding dress.

In October 1929, the world was shaken by the Wall Street Crash, which triggered the collapse of North America's economy and a global financial crisis. In common with other industries, Britain's fashion and textiles trades suffered a downturn in sales as people from all ranks of society were forced to retrench. British *Vogue*'s dressmaking supplements in the early years of the 1930s recommended wedding costumes that were plain, simple and adaptable. White satin, which could be dyed after the wedding, was the fabric of choice and trimmings were limited to machine lace sleeves, collar details and perhaps a bolero. A train could be remade into a short evening coat or, if it was an extension of the dress, cut off and made into a cape.[15]

SOCIETY WEDDINGS

In spite of, or perhaps because of the hard times, many people continued to be fascinated by the apparently charmed lives of the rich and famous. Margaret Whigham (later Duchess of Argyll, 1912–93) was a wealthy, green-eyed society beauty who loved the camera and gossip columns as much as they loved her. Though she denied that her father had employed a press agent for her, she acknowledged the importance of the leading gossip columnists, Don (the Marquis of Donegal), Valentine (Viscount Castlerosse) and William Hickey (Tom Driberg) to creating and sustaining her image as one of the most beautiful and fascinating women of her generation.[16] When she married Charles Sweeny (1909–93), a Roman Catholic, Irish-American amateur golfer and stockbroker with matinée idol looks on 21 February 1933, her fans brought traffic to a standstill outside the Brompton Oratory in London. Film of the wedding shows a sea of people jostling with photographers and police to catch a glimpse of the bride and her nine attendants.[17]

Margaret Whigham's dress (pls 1–2) was made by the young London designer Norman Hartnell

(1901–79), whose romantic evening and special occasion wear fused the British love affair with the picturesque with the chic sophistication that typified 1930s style. He created a svelte ivory satin sheath dress which was moulded to the body, flared at the knee into deep tulle panels and had dramatic medieval-style hanging sleeves. The skirt of the dress extends into a twelve-foot train designed to make the maximum impact in the impressive aisle of the church. Dress and train are decorated with embroidered, appliquéd and cut-work orange-flowers embellished with artificial pearls and bugle beads (pl.90). Hartnell had used this style of embroidery and 'angel' sleeves for two earlier wedding dresses, but the dramatic extravagance of Margaret Whigham's gown perfectly reflected her star status.[18] Although a team of thirty worked on the dress for six weeks the bride professed to be outraged by its cost of £52. This was almost equivalent to a year's wages for 17–20-year-old women working in London who earned an average weekly wage of £1 10s.[19] The dress's wedding-specific embroidery and extravagant train which is integral to its design make it an early example of the concept of a dress for a day.

90 Silk wedding dress (detail) by Norman Hartnell, London, 1933. Decorated with the designer's favourite bridal motif of orange flowers, the dress's skirt extended into a twelve-foot train.
V&A: T.836–1974. Given and worn by Margaret, Duchess of Argyll for her first marriage to Mr Charles Sweeny

91 'The Wedding Gown at Last' from Marshall & Snelgrove, *The Wedding of Lucy Fairchild* (London, 1928). In this storybook designed to market the department store, the saleswoman offers impeccable advice to a mother and daughter on stylish yet appropriate garb for the daughter's trousseau and wedding.
Museum of London

THE WEDDING GOWN AT LAST

On 6 November 1934 the Sweenys attended the wedding of their friends Baba Beaton (1912–73) and Alec Hambro (1910–43) at St Mark's Church in North Audley Street, London. Baba's brother, the photographer and designer Cecil Beaton (1904–80), stage-managed the wedding and designed her head-dress (pl.92). The press identified it as a medieval wimple but Beaton claimed to have been inspired by the head-covering worn by nuns under their black hoods. The success of Lady Diana Manners as the Madonna in Max Reinhardt's 1932 stage pro-duction of *The Miracle*, when she was dressed as a nun, and the actress Gwen Ffrangcon-Davies's headdresses in Gordon Daviot's 1933 historical drama *Richard of Bordeaux* had made nuns and wim-ples topical.

The bride's cream silk satin dress is an early example of the work of Charles James (1906–78), a young Anglo-American designer who excelled at cutting and draping (pls 93–4). Every dart and seam was carefully considered to maximize fit while emphasizing the natural sculptural grace of the female body. The fabric is cut on the bias and the dress, which has no fastenings, slips on over the head.[20] Instead of the usual train James extended the flounce at the skirt front into a divided train forming two elegant streamers of fabric. The bride wore a wax orange-blossom choker around the dress's high cowl neck, adding a touch of tradition to James's thoroughly modern interpretation of the white wedding dress. The theatrical spectacle Cecil Beaton created around the wedding also merged tra-dition and modernity. While the church and porch were decorated with Madonna lilies sprayed with crimson paint and red pampas grass, the two page boys who acted as trainbearers were dressed in Eliz-abethan ruffs, red velvet jackets emblazoned with gold braid and white satin breeches.[21] The single bridesmaid was dressed in a red velvet bustle dress and her rose headdress echoed the bride's huge bou-quet of crimson roses.

Victor Stiebel had created a similarly restrained wedding dress for Joan Pearson (b.1912) for her mar-riage to Anthony Acton (d.1993) in 1932, which demonstrates the small-breasted, elongated profile

92 'Medieval wedding', *Pathé Gazette*, 1934. This still from a newsreel shows Baba Beaton and her husband Alec Hambro leaving St Mark's Church, North Audley Street, London, after their wedding.
© British Pathé

that was fashionable in the first half of the 1930s (pls 95–6). When Princess Marina of Greece (1906–68) became engaged to Prince George (1902–42), the handsome and party-loving fourth son of George V, she went to Edward Molyneux for her trousseau and wedding dress. The couturier's nationality made him a patriotic choice, but his position as one of the most prestigious designers in Paris accorded with the princess's reputation for style and elegance. Molyneux's selection of Lyons silk brocade whose design incorporated the English rose acknowledged the quality of French silks and the importance of symbolism to British royal ceremonial. His design for the princess ignored the growing trend for broad shoulders and he created a slim-fitting, loose gown with a cowl neck and wide cuffs. The dress was made in the workrooms of Molyneux's London house in Grosvenor Street and at her wedding the princess looked regal and relaxed (pl.97).

From the mid-1930s shoulders became broader, the bust more prominent and the waist more defined. Sleeves were long and narrow, or full and flared, and hems swept the floor. Women wore their hair away from the forehead to expose the brow and head-dresses were fitted to the crown of the head. Wimples remained popular and in 1936 both Jeanne

93 Silk satin wedding dress (front) by Charles James, London, 1934.
V&A: T.271&A–1974.
Given by Mrs Alec Hambro

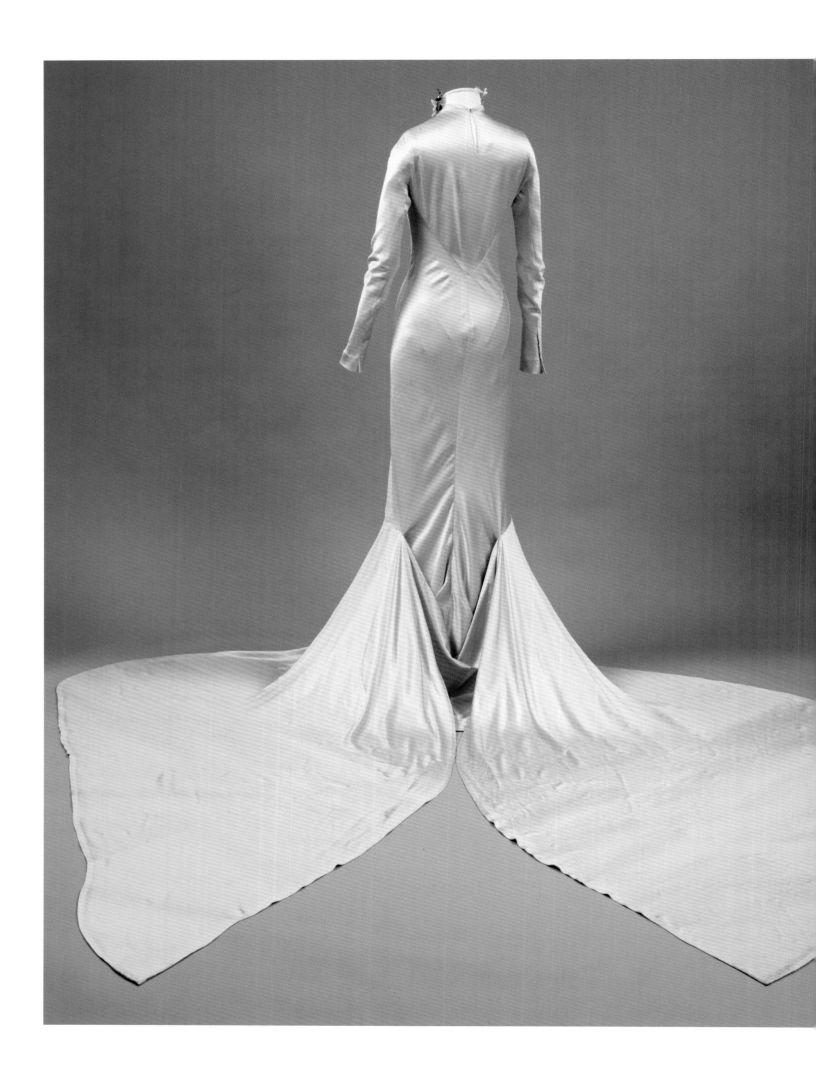

94 Silk satin wedding dress (back)

V&A: T.271&A–1974.
Given by Mrs Alec Hambro

95 Wedding dress design
by Victor Stiebel, pencil drawing, London, 1932. Stiebel won the commission to design Joan Pearson's wedding dress in the year that he opened his fashion house in Bruton Street in London.

V&A: T.73–1966.
Given by Mrs Anthony Acton

96 Joan Pearson, London, 1932. Hand-coloured photograph by Lenare. The bride completed her outfit with a mother-of-pearl sequin cap created by Jeanne Lanvin and a long silk tulle veil.

V&A: T.74–1966.
Given by Mrs Anthony Acton

Lanvin (1867–1946) and Madeleine Vionnet (1876–1975) designed versions of nun-like bridal dresses. Vionnet's was girdled with orange-blossom and the skirt doubled back to become a veil.[22] Dress styles were eclectic but the strongest trends were slim-fitting draped styles inspired by classical and medieval dress or garments that incorporated volume and reflected the influence of Victorian and Edwardian fashions. The success of Hollywood films set in the Victorian period such as *The Barretts of Wimpole Street* (1934) and *David Copperfield* (1935) fuelled the trend and helped to familiarize the public with the new silhouette (pl.98).

Films offered an opportunity for fantasy and escapism, a mood to which *Vogue* turned in 1937 in an article which encouraged brides to act out their fantasies and take full advantage of the opportunity their wedding offered to be a star for the day.

97 Duke of Kent and Princess Marina of Greece, 1934. The couple are shown after their marriage in Westminster Abbey on 29 November.

Photograph: Haynes Archive
© Popperfoto / Getty Images

98 David Copperfield (Frank Lawton) and Dora (Maureen O'Sullivan) at their wedding breakfast. The film of Charles Dickens's novel was MGM's major Christmas release for 1935. Dolly Tree designed the costumes.
MGM / The Kobal Collection

'Splurge' on an expensive outfit ... 'Engrave your-self on the memories of those gathered together.' For a grand wedding they suggested Edward Molyneux's white satin bustle dress with a ruffle collar – 'the whole thing looking as if it might have been lifted out of your grandmother's brass-bound cedar-chest' – or an 'eye-turning' pale, smoke-blue satin dress by Chicago-born designer Mainbocher (Main Rousseau Bocher, 1890–1976), worn with long blue gloves and bluebird pins to hold the veil in place. Hereditary red-heads were urged to 'dramatize it [their hair colour] with a grey wedding, and move down to the altar in a misty chiffon dress of the palest grey', or, 'if the Directoire era has your fancy ... [choose] a slim dress of white crêpe, its skirt rapier-pleated, with Greek scrolls of embroidery at the top.'[23] The article drew attention to the fashionable use of colours other than white for weddings and highlights the growing emphasis on choice in fashion. In 1935 Norman Hart-nell had designed a very pale pearl-pink satin dress for the marriage of Lady Alice Montagu-Douglas-Scott (1901–2004) to Prince Henry, Duke of Gloucester (1900–74), which encouraged brides to think of wearing pink. Wallis Simpson's (1896–1986) light-blue dress, designed by Mainbocher for her third marriage, to the Duke of Windsor (1894–1972) in April 1937, also spawned copies and, as the article in *Vogue* revealed, other blue dresses.

SECOND WORLD WAR BRIDES

A sketch of a bridal outfit from the House of Paquin dating to 1939–40 encapsulates the femininity and coquettishness of fashions at the end of the 1930s (pl.99). Its leg-of-mutton sleeves, pie-crust frills, pinched waist and flaring basque, topped by a seduc-tively tilted hat, conjure up the theatrical glamour that typified the 1930s. In September 1939 Britain declared war on Germany and with the onset of the blitz the following September, when British cities were bombarded by day and night, the war became a bitter reality for the civilian population. While magazines and even the government suggested that keeping up a smart appearance could be important for morale, most women were more concerned with meeting their family's basic clothing needs. Fabric

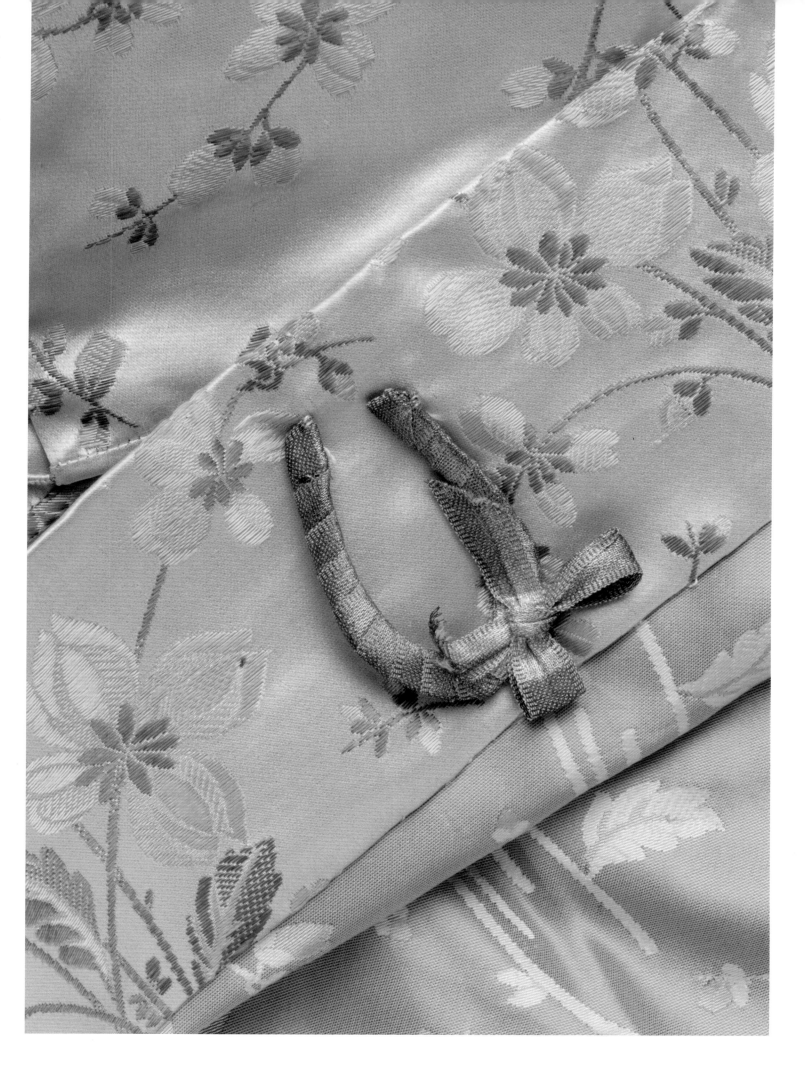

102 Leaving for church,
London, 5 November 1940.
A bride leaves her bombed-
out house for her wedding.
Photograph by Fred Ramage /
Getty Images

shortages and the rising cost of clothing prompted the government to introduce a raft of measures in June 1941 and spring 1942 that were intended to keep prices down, make the most appropriate and economical use of scarce raw materials and ensure a fair distribution of clothing to all. They included rationing and regulations that controlled the manufacture of textiles and clothing at all levels from couture to ready-made.

Brides had to be imaginative and practical. As *Vogue* remarked, 'It behoves a bride to have her head screwed on. Fluttering helplessness is a peace-time luxury'.[24] Some managed to marry in white (pl.102) by altering outfits worn by relatives, borrowing from friends, hiring a dress or making something new from unrationed materials like net curtaining and upholstery fabric.[25] When Elizabeth King (1922–2003) married Ralph Rowland Absalom (1915–2002) on 6 September 1941, she chose a traditional long dress in a colourful fabric (pls 100–101). Having insufficient clothing coupons to purchase a ready-made dress, she bought light-weight upholstery fabric and had it made up by Ella Dolling, a London dressmaker. The dress's sweetheart neckline,

**103 Margaret Harper
and Oliver Spinney**, 1942.
The pockets of the bride's
tailored jacket were designed
to reflect the flap-pockets on
army tunics.
V&A: Furniture, Textiles and
Fashion Archive

slightly puffed sleeves and fitted bodice are typical
of its date. Elizabeth's choice of a fabric patterned
with buttercups reflects her occupation as a florist
and perhaps her enjoyment of simple country flowers and memories of more carefree times. She later
removed the sleeves to make the dress more suitable for evening wear. Other women made dresses
from parachute silk and rayon, salvaged by fiancés
on the battlefield or bought from superfluous stock
at the end of the war. Examples have survived made
from the heavier fabrics used to drop supplies from
aircraft and the lighter silks designed to support
parachutists.

Many women married in their service uniform or
chose a smart suit or afternoon dress. In spring 1942
Margaret Harper (b.1918) wore a blue wool crêpe
tailored dress and matching jacket, trimmed with
grey astrakhan, for her wedding to Oliver Spinney
(1918–2004) at Rowley Regis in the Midlands. The
outfit, purchased from Marshall & Snelgrove, is
practical and stylish. A photograph of the bride and
groom suggests that their outfits were deliberately
chosen, down to their well-polished shoes, to reflect
their partnership and love (pl.103). The fashionable
broad shoulders and flap pockets of Margaret
Harper's jacket and the angle of her pretty hat echo
her husband's uniform while losing none of their
femininity. Hats, which had escaped rationing in
1941, were very popular for wartime brides whatever
costume or colour they chose, providing an unre-
stricted outlet for personal expression.

Bridal fashions in the interwar period demonstrate the continuing appeal of the traditional white
wedding dress and veil. Alternative colours and styles
of headdress were fashionable, but white's adapt-
ability gave it durability. For an era that prized subtle
colours, white's many shades suited a range of com-
plexions and hair colours as well as the eclectic
fashions of the interwar years. Whatever style of wedding dress a bride wanted, medieval or modernist,
classical or high Victorian, it would look appropriate
made in a white fabric. White never went out of fashion and in Britain its links to the wedding ceremony
were now so deeply embedded that for many women
it was the only choice for a bride.

To wed in red

In June 1938, Monica Maurice (1908–95) married Dr Arthur Newton Jackson in a quiet ceremony at the Chapel of Our Lady on Rotheram Bridge in South Yorkshire. Monica Maurice was an independent, unconventional woman who in 1938 become the first – and until 1978 only – woman member of the Association of Mining Electrical Engineers. She had a passion for racing cars and flying, and loved clothes. Red was one of her favourite colours, making her choice of a ruby-coloured silk gauze mid-calf dress for her wedding quite personal (pl.104). With its contrasting deep-blue belt and buttons, and worn over a matching red artificial silk slip, it was a feminine and fashionable dress perfectly suited to her petite frame. She wore a short shoulder-length veil and flowered wreath.

Rachel Ginsburg (1923–2010) also chose a wedding outfit in red. She wore a tailored wool skirt-suit when she married Walter Foster, a fellow student at the London School of Economics, at Brondesbury Synagogue in London, on 4 January 1949 (pl.105). Resources remained low after the Second World War, making new clothes difficult to acquire. The bride found this suit with the help of her aunt in the Bon Marché department store in Liverpool, where her family lived. Although the original designer is unknown, the extremely fashionable outfit was probably a model from a British couture or high-quality ready-to-wear house. The deep, flared peplum and nipped-in waist of the jacket reflect the 'New Look' popularized by Parisian couturier Christian Dior in 1947. As clothing rationing, introduced in June 1941, would not end until March 1949, the bride's fellow students donated clothing coupons to support the £22 purchase. Although expensive at a time when a female insurance clerk in Liverpool earned £2.30–£4.70 a week, its fashionable cut and good-quality fabrics would have remained smart for several years, and the jacket and skirt could be worn separately with different garments.[1] While Rachel's mother felt a vivid red suit was a little daring for a bride to wear to a traditionally modest synagogue ceremony, her father and fiancé both approved.

Both these wedding outfits offer a surprising contrast with the popular contemporary image of the bride as a young woman in virginal white, which was widely disseminated in the media and through Hollywood films. While there was a vogue in the 1920s and 1930s for delicately coloured bridal gowns, stronger colours still made a bold statement. For the bride conditioned to think in terms of the traditional Western white-wedding, red is one of the most daring alternatives. But for many non-Western cultures, it is a traditional colour for wedding garments. Red is often worn by Hindu and Muslim brides, and is also favoured by Chinese and Vietnamese brides for whom it represents good luck.

Daniel Milford-Cottam

104 Silk gauze wedding dress with artificial silk slip, British, 1938.
V&A: T.716:1 to 3–1995.
Worn by Miss Monica Maurice and given by her family

105 Wool wedding suit trimmed with black silk braid, purchased at Bon Marché, Liverpool, British, 1948.
V&A: T.14&A–1960.
Given by Mrs W. Foster

READY-TO-WEAR

1945–90

In the decades that followed the Second World War, couture's dominance of the high-fashion market was successfully challenged by high-quality, innovative ready-to-wear designed for young, affluent consumers. Although Paris reasserted its influence over high fashion immediately after the war, from the 1960s a wave of young British ready-to-wear designers established London as an alternative fashion centre for cutting-edge design. They changed Britain's international fashion profile and brought fresh approaches to bridal wear.

White was the dominant colour for wedding dresses throughout the period. Bridal fashions at first followed contemporary fashion and until the 1970s were made in day and evening lengths. During the 1970s, the political, economic and social upheavals of the decade were reflected in a proliferation of sub-cultural styles and widely varying approaches to fashion. Bridal designers largely took their cue from the vogue for romantic styles of dress inspired by every era from the Victorian period through to the 1940s. This trend became increasingly exaggerated. By the 1980s, it led to designs based more in fantasy than fashion, which had little use after the wedding, and commentators suggested that bridal wear was becoming fossilized. However the 1980s also saw Britain benefit once again from a new generation of talented designers who created custom-made wedding dresses for brides with more avant-garde taste. Film remained an important medium for communicating new fashions and the resumption and rapid expansion of television broadcasting after the war brought it into homes across the country.

COUTURE BRIDAL WEAR, 1945–60

The Second World War ended on 2 September 1945. The British fashion industry had hoped that the war would reduce Paris's dominance of the international fashion market, but the success of the debut collection of Christian Dior (1905–57) in February 1947 re-established the city's pre-war reputation as the creative force behind women's fashion. Ernestine Carter, fashion editor of the magazine *Harper's Bazaar*, attended Dior's first show and recalled the overwhelmingly positive response to 'the contrast of the discipline of the fitted bodices with tiny wasp waists and the billowing grace of the full skirts, the softly curved shoulders and nonchalant back-dipping, open collar'.[1] Dior's silhouette, which he described as the *Corolle* line, essentially refined and re-presented the hour-glass fashions that had been popular in the late 1930s. The style, which the press hailed as the 'New Look', influenced fashion for a decade.

Britain, burdened with national debt, remained in the grip of austerity. Cloth and clothing were in short supply and clothes rationing remained in place until 15 March 1949. The British government was horrified by the quantity of fabric required for the longer-length full skirts and branded the style unpatriotic and inappropriate. Women, longing for an end to years of thrift and 'making do', were seduced by its novelty, luxury and femininity and many responded by lengthening their skirts. London's couturiers followed Dior's lead, but the British version of the New Look was more restrained. It emphasized the bust and hips but the waist, although appearing small, was less cinched and there was a noticeable resistance to the sloping shoulder line.

When Princess Elizabeth (b.1926), the future Queen Elizabeth II, became engaged to Lieutenant Philip Mountbatten (b.1921) in July 1947, Norman Hartnell was asked to make her wedding dress.[2] This most prestigious of commissions confirmed the designer's position as London's leading couturier. Recognizing the central role that the dress would play in the wedding's pageantry, Hartnell based his design loosely on the figure of Flora in Sandro Botticelli's painting *La Primavera* (*c*.1482). The goddess's dress is sprinkled and garlanded with flowers symbolizing love and the advent of spring and Hartnell saw a parallel in the princess's marriage which brought a promise of renewal and recovery from the pain and deprivation of war. He chose traditional floral motifs to decorate the satin dress and fifteen-foot court train, including roses, orange-blossom and sprays of corn, which are emblematic of love and fertility. The wedding dress has square shoulders, a fitted bodice which defines the curve of waist without suppressing it, a shaped neckline and long

slim sleeves. Its skirt, which is cut on the cross, falls from a low pointed waist into a deep circular train. Cecil Beaton's portrait of the twenty-one-year-old princess shows how Hartnell's design skilfully blended formality, freshness and youth (pl.106).

A fashionable wedding allowed a more modish interpretation of the new style. The silhouette and flattering off-shoulder collar of Patricia Cunningham's (1921–2007) 1948 wedding dress reflected the graceful sophistication of the New Look (pl.107). The bride, a *Vogue* model who became the magazine's fashion editor in 1951, asked Edward Molyneux to design her dress for her marriage to couturier Charles Creed (1906–66). Her future husband was born in Paris and worked there for his family's couture house, Henry Creed & Company, until 1940 when he and Molyneux fled to Britain following the German occupation of the city.[3] Molyneux had returned to France in 1945 and the bride's white watered silk gown was made in the workrooms of his London fashion house. The dress's sophisticated elegance and impeccable craftsmanship are typical of the designer's aesthetic.

In the early 1950s British *Vogue* identified two styles of wedding dress: the traditional, made of 'ivory satin, full length, sweepingly full', worn with a tiara and long tulle veil or family lace, and the new, youthful, bouffant 'short, formal wedding dress', 'tipping the ankles', created in diaphanous, crisp fabrics like organdie, lace and chiffon.[4] When Hermione Wills (b.1926) married Mervyn Evans at St Mark's Church in North Audley Street, London on 23 July 1951, she chose a traditional dress designed by Norman Hartnell. Her mother was a friend of the designer and director of his company, making him a natural choice. Hartnell excelled at special occasion dresses incorporating embroidery and Hermione Wills's dress is typical of his approach. The dress was designed to reflect her personality, flatter her figure and add grace and dignity to her appearance as she made her entrance as a bride. The lustrous pearl-coloured silk is a perfect foil for the bands of floral embroidery which sweep down from below the breastbone to circle the back of the trained skirt (pls 108–10).

109 Embroidered silk wedding dress (back)

V&A: T.217&A–1972.
Given by Mrs H.S. Ball

110 Hermione Wills and Mervyn Evans on their wedding day, London, 23 July 1951.

Photograph by Lenare.
V&A: Furniture, Textiles and Fashion Archive

READY-TO-WEAR

During the 1950s the number of British women with the income, time and inclination to patronize London's couture houses diminished. The city's leading couturiers belonged to the Incorporated Society of London Fashion Designers (1942–70).[5] Collectively the group was reluctant to accept the changes taking place in British society. They failed to engage with new ideas about fashion and a new generation of young, opinionated consumers, and their client base shrank. Young designers also turned their back on couture, believing that the future of fashion lay with high-quality, innovative ready-to-wear. Although some of the most successful were self-taught, many were educated in art colleges which, unlike the pre-war technical schools, now taught creative fashion design. Faced

with their success many couturiers retired but a few, like Norman Hartnell and Hardy Amies (1909–2003), who also designed for the royal family, had more sustainable businesses. They were joined by a small group of young designers with couture workrooms who designed for the tastes and lifestyle of their generation. They included Bellville Sassoon – the successful design partnership of Belinda Bellville (b.1930) and David Sassoon (b.1932) – Bruce Oldfield (b.1950) and Victor Edelstein (b.1946). Bridal wear was one of the most important facets of their businesses as dressing the bride might lead to providing her trousseau and dressing other members of her family. Both couturiers and designers provided direction and inspiration for the ready-to-wear bridal companies which supplied department stores and bridal shops.

A miracle of transformation has been performed by John Cavanagh of London, with his enchanting wedding dress. A button-through over-blouse is slipped under the cummerbund—which is cleverly attached to the all-in-one dress—and the most demure and pretty bride will walk up the aisle in full-skirted simplicity. Remove the blouse and there is the most romantic evening dress with a butterfly bow at the back, whose ends trail to the hem. "Satin Venus" Courtaulds fabric, exclusive to Jacqmar, was used in this dress. The pearl-embroidered head-dress is by Madge Chard over a Witchcraft tulle veil. This pattern, cut to your own measurements, costs one guinea as a Model "Special" Pattern—or 8s. cut in stock sizes as a Model "Standard" Pattern.

Further details on page 114

Model Pattern No. 194

A John Cavanagh Model to Make

Britain was well-known for its high-quality ready-to-wear companies which employed well-trained in-house designers and copied models purchased from couture houses in Paris and London. Ready-to-wear wedding outfits were available from department stores, the salons of bridal wear companies and bridal boutiques, all of which offered specialist advice, fitters and an alteration service. Some sold models that could be made to the client's measurements alongside off-the-peg styles. Bridal wear companies included Mercia – at the top end of the market, with a salon in Cavendish Place in central London and sold through 'exclusive' outlets throughout the country – and Roecliff & Chapman, who offered more accessibly priced dresses made from man-made fibres. Versatility remained important as Britain inched towards economic recovery and most wedding dresses were evening styles which could be worn afterwards, sold with a matching bolero or jacket to cover the décolletage and arms during the wedding ceremony.

Horrockses Fashions employed talented young designers to create fashionable, high-quality garments from its parent company's cotton. They made a limited range of bridal dresses and in 1951 *Vogue* featured a white piqué Horrockses dress which they recommended for brides on a budget.[6] Throughout the 1950s the Cotton Board's Colour, Design and Style Centre worked with leading ready-to-wear manufacturers and London's couturiers to promote the use of cotton in high fashion. Some fashion shows benefited from the occasional involvement of 'celebrity' mannequins who took part because the show featured couture. In 1953 Myrtle Crawford modelled a wedding dress designed by Hardy Amies made of white cotton organdie and poplin (pl.111). Designers had used cotton for evening resort wear in the 1930s, but its promotion as a fashionable fabric for weddings was a post-war development.

Women with access to television sets could watch the Cotton Board's fashion shows on television from 1951. By 1955 a television service was available to 94% of the British population, and within nine years television ownership was reaching saturation point.[7] Television was a major addition to

the existing methods of disseminating information. Fashion magazines of course remained an important medium for brides-to-be looking for ideas, and most devoted a few pages to bridal wear in their February or April issues. *Woman's Journal*, which had a broad middle-class readership, offered a wedding dress pattern created by a British or French designer each year. The pattern could be cut by hand to the measurements of the wearer for a guinea (£1 1s) or purchased as a standard pattern for 7s 6d. In 1955 women bank workers earned an annual salary of about £192 at sixteen-years-old rising to £305 at twenty-one, with a ceiling of £452 at thirty-one. This suggests that the standard dress pattern was easily affordable for a young woman in a good job.[8]

The principal cost of a dress lay in its fabric. Most of the fabrics recommended for the patterns were man-made and some patterns promoted particular manufacturers. In 1956 John Cavanagh (1914–2003), a talented Irish couturier who had worked for Molyneux and Pierre Balmain (1914–82) before setting up his London house in 1951, designed a dress and over-blouse for the magazine (pl.112). It was photographed made up in Courtauld's man-made fabric 'satin Venus' which was exclusive to the British textile manufacturer Jacqmar. The metres of fabric required to create the fashionable full skirts made silk very costly. The new generation of 'miracle' man-made fibres offered a cheaper alternative and the industry in Britain and the USA poured money into promoting nylon, acrylic and polyester as new, modern fabrics that were equal to or improved on natural raw materials. In 1955 *Brides* magazine, which targeted a middle-class readership, was launched in Britain. Published quarterly, it was the country's first magazine dedicated to weddings.

In the second half of the 1950s shorter wedding dresses became increasingly popular for brides who considered themselves young and up-to-date. The style was also ideal for brides who wanted a dress that they could wear on semi-formal occasions after the wedding. In 1956 *Harper's Bazaar* characterized the ballet-length (mid-calf) dress as the career girl's choice.[9] Screen actress Grace Kelly wore a ballet-length embroidered white organdie wedding dress designed by the MGM costume designer Helen Rose (1904–85) in her role as Tracy Lord in the musical film *High Society* (1956). The film coincided with the star's fairytale engagement to Prince Rainier of Monaco, making the style particularly romantic for her female fans. Plainer, more sculptural ankle-length styles in stiffer fabrics offered an alternative to full, soft, shorter skirts. These styles could be worn after the wedding for evening occasions.

By 1957 Europe's economy had recovered. In Britain, full employment, rising wages and a marked improvement to the standard of living led Prime Minister Harold Macmillan to claim that most of Britain had 'never had it so good'. In London, the buoyant economy fuelled the rise of a wave of young entrepreneurs and taste-makers who would transform the capital into a city whose image was young, fashionable and anti-establishment. However weddings continued to be formal family occasions. In 1959 70% of people married in church and most chose traditional white weddings.[10]

1960S COUTURE AND READY-TO-WEAR

On 6 May 1960 Princess Margaret (1930–2002) married the photographer Antony Armstrong-Jones (b.1930) at Westminster Abbey. It was the first British royal wedding service to be televised and broadcast live across Europe. A new zoom lens enabled millions of people to see the royal couple in close up.[11] The bride's simple white organza wedding dress was created by Norman Hartnell. It enhanced the presence of the princess without overwhelming her petite figure and is one of the designer's most successful bridal dresses (pl.113). The wedding generated intense public interest and good-humoured celebrations, prompting the *Economist* to reflect on the far greater attention paid by the British public, 'and especially the women of Britain', to the wedding than to politics: 'The decorations and the fairy glitter from the evening floodlights, and the magic televised moments of the wedding day, will live on long after drearier political moments are forgotten, in the impressionable subconsciousness of the superficially blasé as well as in the open memories of ordinary and livelier people.'[12]

Young designers in the 1960s wanted to design bridal wear that acknowledged the solemnity of the wedding, but was youthful. When Mary Quant (b.1934) was asked to create a pattern for *Woman's Journal* for February 1960, she offered a white sleeveless dress with a slim-fitting bodice and a stiff, mid-calf-length, bell-shaped skirt. A large tailored bow decorated the waist and a similar bow held the model's short tulle veil in place.[13] The designer, who had attended London's Goldsmiths College of Art, was one of the most high-profile members of the 'Chelsea Set' who helped to change the way fashion was designed and sold. Quant, who was self-taught as a fashion designer, realized that the future of fashion lay in innovative ready-to-wear, sold in less formal, more stimulating retail spaces.

Millinery was promoted as a youthful alternative to the traditional veil and wreath in the 1960s. For autumn 1961 the cover of *Brides* magazine featured a made-to-measure satin pillbox hat trimmed with a puff of ostrich feathers (pl.114). Its designer was Belinda Bellville. Custom-made wedding dresses

113 **Princess Margaret and Antony Armstrong-Jones, 1st Earl of Snowdon** on their wedding day, Buckingham Palace, 6 May 1960. The bride's white organza wedding dress was created by Norman Hartnell. Her veil, made by the Parisian milliner Claude St Cyr to Hartnell's design, was held in place by the Poltimore tiara.

Photograph by Cecil Beaton. V&A: PH.3341–1987. © Cecil Beaton / V&A Images

Brides

2/6

were a Bellville Sassoon speciality and by the early
1960s they accounted for at least a quarter of their
business. In 1961 they were invited to design ready-
to-wear bridal collections for Woollands, a
Knightsbridge department store that was being
transformed into London's leading retailer of avant-
garde British fashion. The same issue of *Brides*
featured an organza headdress by James Wedge
(b.1939), who had studied at Walthamstow Art College and designed hats for Mary Quant, and a gold
skullcap by Gavin Waddell, a graduate of Saint Martin's School of Art, who had his own label.

When the jeweller Wendy Ramshaw (b.1939)
married David Watkins (b.1940) at Christ Church in
Sunderland on 12 August 1962, she wore a short
pearl-studded veil trimmed with white artificial roses
and ribbons, with a short dress. The bride, a graduate of Newcastle College of Art and Industrial
Design, met her future husband at a party when she
was studying for an Art Teacher's Diploma at Reading University. Both became internationally
acclaimed jewellers. The dresses Ramshaw designed
for herself and her two college-friend bridesmaids
were influenced by the styles worn by the French
actress and sex symbol Brigitte Bardot (b.1934). Bardot had married Jacques Charrier in 1959 in a short,
girlish, pink and white check dress designed by couturier Jacques Esterel (1918–74). Wendy Ramshaw
chose a firm white fabric with a satin stripe which was
made up by a local dressmaker and trimmed with
pleated white satin (pl.115). David Watkins wore a
dark lounge suit – a popular alternative to the traditional morning coat. The sketch of the dresses,
whose design she modified after she chose the mate-

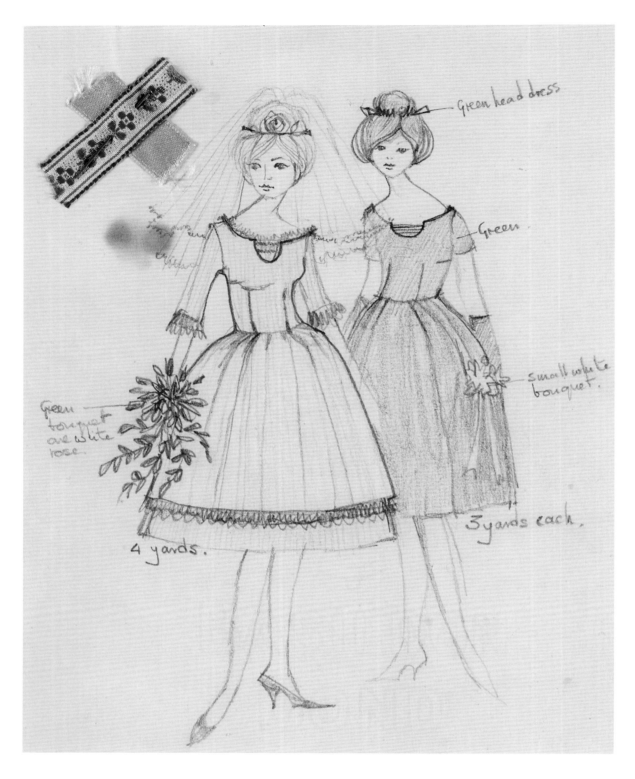

Green head dress

Green.

Green bouquet over white rose.

small white bouquet.

4 yards.

3 yards each.

116 Sketch of a wedding dress and bridesmaid's dress by Wendy Ramshaw, pencil drawing with fabric swatches, Britain, 1962.

© Wendy Ramshaw

rial for her dress, includes ideas for bouquets (pl.116). Ramshaw did not want the standard florist's bridal bouquets and in spite of her mother's reservations she insisted on making them herself from flowers gathered in her parents' garden.[14]

More traditional full-length wedding dresses remained popular. Their silhouette had evolved from the late 1950s to become quite flat and rigid at the front with the volume and drapery behind, so that from the side the dress resembled a triangle. Actress April Olrich's (b.1933) ivory shantung wedding dress worn in 1963 is typical of the elegant simplicity of this style (pl.117). It was designed by Jacques Heim (1899–1967) of Paris and bought off-the-peg. Heim's garments were made under licence in London for sale in British boutiques and department stores. The dress has a fitted boned bodice with a wide scooped neckline, three-quarter-length raglan sleeves and a full-length A-line skirt which is trained at the back. While the front is completely plain, the centre back neckline is decorated with a bow whose ends extend into interlined panels to form a train. Instead of a bouquet, the bride carried her mother's prayer book with satin ribbons trailing from it.

117 Shantung silk wedding dress by Jacques Heim, made in London, 1963. Despite changes in fashion, full-length traditional wedding dresses remained popular.

V&A: T.404:1, 2–2001.
Given by April Olrich

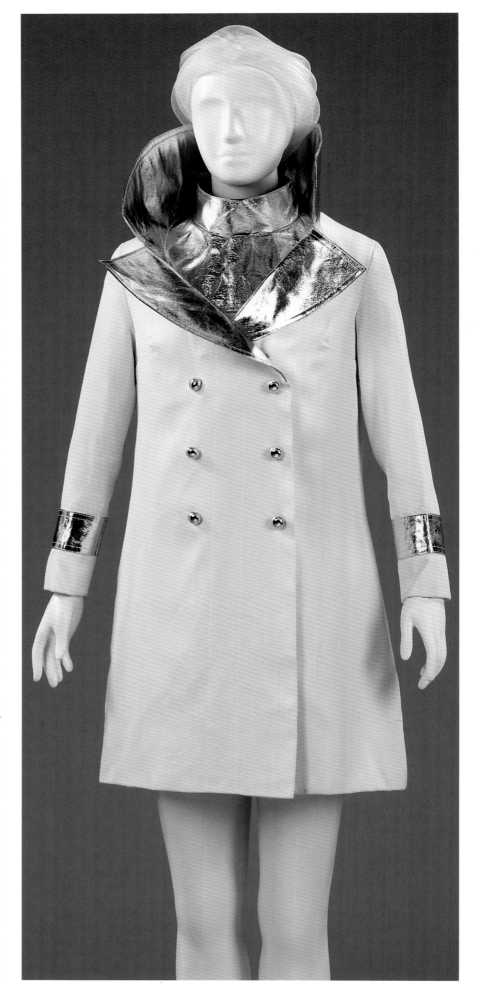

118 Cotton gabardine coat and mini-dress by John Bates for his Jean Varon label, London, 1966. Fashion journalist Marit Allen wore this outfit when she married film producer Sandy Lieberson.
V&A: T.261:1, 2–2009

During the 1960s the institution of marriage was questioned in progressive circles. *Nova*, launched in 1965 as a 'new kind of magazine for a new kind of woman … for women who make up their own minds', published regular articles about marriage and its challenges. Yet its approach to the topic was ambiguous. In June 1965 a critical article arguing that marriage could not sustain love was nevertheless accompanied in the magazine by a feature on wedding fashions. The sartorial advice was pragmatic. Having got to the altar, a bride should aim for a look that was 'totally traditional, absolutely pretty, the maximum in flattery … it's how you're going to be remembered for years and years. It is wise, therefore, to play it safe.' Both the illustrated dresses, which have wide necklines and long sleeves, fall loosely from the shoulders to the ground. One, 'Saint Laurent-inspired', made in satin and available from Liberty's, is severely plain apart from a single large bow above the breast bone; the other, in shantung silk, has a heavy train and is scattered with fabric flowers. The same flowers decorate the 'Victorian-heroine snood' worn with the dress.[15] The models look pale, soulful and hollow-eyed, in contrast to the natural look that *Vogue* recommended in the mid-1960s. Like the dresses, which hid the female curves, their appearance references the anti-fashion styles and unconventional attitudes associated with women moving in bohemian, artistic circles in the mid-nineteenth century.

By 1966 hemlines for daywear were well above the knee. When Marit Allen (1941–2007), editor of the 'Young Ideas' pages at British *Vogue*, became engaged to the film producer Sandy Lieberson (b.1936), she asked John Bates (b.1938), whom she believed to be one of the decade's most significant and free-thinking designers, to make her wedding outfit. Bates created a mini-length, white cotton gabardine, sleeveless shift dress with a silvered yoke and stand collar. Its matching double-breasted coat is trimmed with silvered dome-shaped buttons, silver bands around the cuffs and a collar with wide lapels (pl.118). The bare-headed bride wore the collar up to frame her face (pl.119). While the 1960s witnessed rapid social change and increasing economic, political and sexual freedom for women, most

bridal wear, whatever the height of the hemline, retained a degree of formality. Bates's conventional combination of a coordinating dress and coat made a very fashionable outfit that was still appropriate, in spite of its shortness, for a church wedding.

The 1960s also offered men opportunities for dressing up. While motley vintage and ethnic clothes, and body-conscious new garments made in colourful and unconventional fabrics could be bought in Chelsea's boutiques, a new generation of tailor/designers set up in Mayfair. Charles Lucas (b.1943) went to Mr Fish in Clifford Street for a suit for his marriage to Antoinette von Westenholz on 9 November 1967. As the bride was a Roman Catholic and the groom a Buddhist, they married at the Church of the Immaculate Conception in Farm Street which allowed mixed-faith weddings. Lucas chose a single-breasted grey cloth suit, which he wore with a white satin cravat.[16] Its jacket has a Regency-style stand collar and lapels. Pop interpretations of nineteenth-century styles and fabrics were a feature of the late 1960s and early 1970s. They

reflected a subversive if romantic engagement with British heritage, which manifested itself in an element of fancy dress even in 'serious' clothes.[17]

In the late 1960s maxi-coats were fashionable and designers offered them as bridal wear (pl.120). In 1968 Belinda Bellville designed a romantic, Russian-style cream silk cloqué coat with a detachable collar and hood trimmed with Arctic fox fur (pl.121). It was inspired by a coat worn by Lara in David Lean's 1965 film *Dr Zhivago*. *The Lady* magazine featured the coat in October 1968 and it was purchased for a wedding that took place at the end of December. Bellville et Cie was set up in 1953 by the recently married Belinda Whately (née Bellville). In 1958 she recruited David Sassoon, a graduate of the prestigious Fashion Design School at London's Royal College of Art, as her assistant. Eventual business partners, by 1970 they had created Bellville Sassoon, a thriving modern couture house. Sassoon attributed their success to tapping 'into the need for well-cut, well-made, flattering clothes for a fashion-forward, moneyed set who wanted couture, but not

120 Zibeline wedding coat-dress by Jean Patou, with shoes by Andrea for Patou, Paris, 1967.

London College of Fashion. The Woolmark Company

121 Silk and fox fur wedding coat by Bellville et Cie, London, 1968. The coat reflects the new fashion for maxi-coats. A fur-trimmed coat worn by Julie Christie as Lara in David Lean's popular film *Dr Zhivago* (1965) inspired its design.

V&A: T.82–1988.

123 Wool wedding dress
by Jean Muir, London, 1969. The design of the braid on the bodice is based on Celtic scrollwork. The inclusion of a blue ribbon and silver horseshoe on the inside hem is also traditional. The dress was worn with shoes by the Italian firm Dal Co.
V&A: T.268–1986. Worn and given by Pamela, Lady Harlech

in a stiff, stuffy way . . . It was the art of clothes to get you noticed.'[18] The pop star Lulu (b.1948) also chose a long white mink-trimmed coat to wear over her white silk mini-dress and boots when she married the musician Maurice Gibb (1949–2003) of the Bee Gees at St James's Church in Gerrards Cross in February 1969 (pl.122). Although it was only a small family wedding, around 1000 people, mainly women and girls, besieged the church to catch sight of the stars.

By the end of the 1960s wedding dresses, like fashion in general, tended to be girlish and pretty, and a renewed interest in historical styles manifested itself in lace, tucks, frills and flounces. Pamela Talmey Colin (b.1934), a former London editor of American *Vogue*, rejected this trend when she married Lord Harlech (1918–85) in London on 11 December 1969. He had served as British Ambassador in Washington during the Kennedy administration, and the bride and groom were a powerful and glamorous couple. Colin commissioned her white wool, high-waisted wedding dress from Jean Muir (1928–95), one of London's most respected ready-to-wear designers. Its considered proportions, clean lines and impeccable finish are typical of Muir's understated approach and meticulous attention to detail. The bold Celtic scrollwork, worked in braid on the front of the dress, probably alludes to the groom's Welsh title (pl.123). The bride's dark hair was dressed around a cluster of long cream passementerie tassels created by the London milliner Graham Smith (b.1938).

1970S WEDDING STYLE

In 1970 the magazine *Queen* announced the arrival of the seventies bride, 'a person not just a fashion cipher, part of a tradition but very much herself'. Instead of 1960s-style white PVC and tight white boots, she would wear 'cloudy organza', a 'great Gainsborough' hat and 'little rosetted shoes echo[ing] a rosetted bodice and skirt'.[19] Fashions rarely take a radical change of direction with the advent of a new decade and the trend for historical styles of wedding dress which were popular in 1970s had appeared in the late 1960s. The flamboyance of sixties fashions also appealed to the new decade and glamorous, overtly sexual clothes provided a contrast with retro-fashion fantasies.

Both approaches were seen at the wedding of Bianca Perez Morena de Macias (b.1945) to the pop star Mick Jagger (b.1943) in Saint-Tropez in 1971 (pl.124). The bride, who was expecting their child, wore a rose-trimmed, white picture hat with a tulle veil and an ankle-length plain white linen skirt-suit designed by Yves Saint Laurent. Although her outfit appeared demure, her jacket revealed her bra-less cleavage. The Rolling Stones front man wore a pale-green, tight-fitting three-piece suit with an open-necked floral shirt and sneakers which lent his appearance an air of easy sexuality. His suit had been made by Nutter's of Savile Row which was founded by Tommy Nutter (1943–92) and Edward Sexton (b.1942) in 1969. Nutter was a supremely confident stylist, Sexton a skilled cutter, and their celebrity clientele included aristocrats and rock stars. Nutter often combined a slim-fitting jacket with wide lapels, and in 1973 *Country Life* featured an eau-de-nil gabardine three-piece wedding suit with a double-breasted frock coat featuring sweeping lapels. The lapels, and the shawl collar of the scoop-necked waistcoat, were faced with watered silk.[20] The suit's exaggerated cut, watered-silk facings and unusual colour created a theatrical pastiche – a traditional wedding style redesigned for the modern dandy.

The sexual revolution of the 1960s became a mass phenomenon in the 1970s. Yet in spite of more young people cohabiting, rising divorce rates and the decline in religious observances, church weddings remained popular.[21] In 1976 Prudence Glynn, fashion editor of *The Times*, bewailed the absurdity of contemporary wedding dress, noting that as marriage had become less crucial to social acceptability, marriage fashions were increasingly divorced from current styles: 'Most modern wedding dresses are pure costume. The cheapness of clothes and the facility of hiring have made them not so much a wardrobe investment as a chance for a once in a life-time chance to dream. Tudor maids, medieval chatelaines with wimple, trouser suits, see-through nymphs by Saint Laurent, all have been suggested for, or actually tripped their way to, the marriage vows with benefit of clergy'.[22]

Fashion was confusing in the 1970s and many of its underlying themes did not accord with traditional ideas of bridal dress. Some fashions like the trouser suit had a masculine edge, others were too revealing, making historical revival styles the most popular bridal choice. Glynn admired independence and originality, and in the 1970s she championed the British designer Zandra Rhodes (b.1940), who was a graduate of the Royal College of Art. Rhodes was a print designer who overcame her ignorance of cut and construction by experimenting with fabric to find forms and techniques that reflected the spirit of her prints. In 1976 she designed a wedding dress for Elizabeth Weiner (b.1953) who, like her fiancé David Emanuel (b.1952), was a fashion student at the Royal College of Art (pl.125). The silk chiffon is printed with a pattern of waves and fronded palms, whose movement and structure are reflected in the narrow pleating on the bodice and skirt and the undulating frills around the waist, which are weighted with tiny gleaming pearls. The iridescent, tinted flower and leaf shapes that decorate the bodice add a fairy sparkle to the matt chiffon. The following year Rhodes designed a provocative wedding dress that translated the aggressive ripped clothes and body piercings of London's punks into a cream silk jersey gown fastened with jewelled safety pins (pl.126). The trained under-dress has a high side-split and its fabric, which has been shredded, holed and peeled away, is pinned and bound with chains. The dress, a blend of punk and goddess,

124 Bianca and Mick Jagger, 12 May 1971. The couple were married in a civil ceremony followed by a religious service in St Anne's Chapel in Saint-Tropez in the south of France.

Photo by Express / Getty Images

pure silk chiffon printed
white on white
fine fine pleat p.
tiny waist tied with
satin band with lovely
bow at back.
Pearled, pleated
frill above the
waist.

125 Sketch of Elizabeth Weiner's wedding dress by Zandra Rhodes, pencil and body colour, London, 1976.
V&A: E.257–2008. Given by Elizabeth Emanuel. © Zandra Rhodes

126 Silk jersey wedding dress by Zandra Rhodes, London, 1977. The publicity generated by Rhodes's provocative punk wedding dress boosted sales of her punk collection.
Zandra Rhodes Archive, Fashion and Textile Museum

illustrates Rhodes's masterful control of fabric and her swift, shrewd commercialization of a contemporary phenomenon that shocked and intimidated. The wedding dress proved a successful marketing tool for the designer's 'posh punk' clothes, which sold particularly well in the USA.

THE 1980S AND THE FAIRYTALE BRIDE

The 1980s have become associated with glamour and excess. Clothes for day and evening were brash and exaggerated. Hour-glass silhouettes, flounced bustles mounted on satin sheath dresses and figure-hugging dresses narrowing to fishtail skirts – all popular styles for formal evening wear in the 1980s – were translated into bridal wear in white taffeta, satin and lace, perpetuating the trend for historical styles while nodding to the latest fashions. In the early 1980s bridal wear was stereotypically feminine and a fitted bodice, tiny waist, full sleeves and sweeping skirts were the dominant look. Dresses individualized with old lace and vintage trimmings were popular and if there was no family veil, an antique one could be bought at Liberty's or from a vintage clothing shop. Lady Diana Spencer's (1961–97) choice of this style of dress for her wedding to Charles, Prince of Wales (b.1948) in July 1981, made it particularly desirable.

David and Elizabeth Emanuel, who had launched their fashion house in 1977, unexpectedly received the coveted commission to design the wedding dress. They had a reputation for making glamorous and revealing evening wear, but their aim was to transform the bride into 'a fairy princess'.[23] As the Princess of Wales stepped from the glass coach outside St Paul's Cathedral two months later, watched by 500 million television viewers across the world, it was generally agreed that the designers had realized their vision.[24] The full skirt and sleeves of the ivory silk taffeta dress and its twenty-five foot train, edged with sparkling beaded lace, added drama and substance to the princess's appearance as she walked down the aisle of the cathedral as a bride and then emerged through its massive columns on the arm of her husband (pl.127). The bride's face and bare neck, unencumbered by jewellery, were

framed by a double-ruffled collar of pearl-encrusted lace set over ivory taffeta. Her veil, held in place by the Spencer family tiara, and the antique panels of lace on the bodice of her dress, twinkled and glistened with hand-embroidered pearls and mother-of-pearl sequins. The dress's delicacy of detail and colour, and its magical, romantic femininity, created a vision of the Princess of Wales that became embedded in the collective memory.[25] The demand for dresses inspired by the royal wedding gown continued well into the mid-1980s, when the vogue for the now derided style was overtaken by a slimmer silhouette with the volume caught at the back of the skirt and more defined shoulders.[26]

In the boom years of the mid-1980s, London fashion enjoyed a particularly vibrant and creative period and its younger designers won an international reputation for their unorthodox and individualistic approach. They worked outside the commercial mainstream and brought their own aes-

127 The Prince and Princess of Wales leave St Paul's Cathedral on their wedding day, 29 July 1981. David and Elizabeth Emanuel designed the Princess's dress.

Photograph: Jayne Fincher / Princess Diana Archive / Getty Images

with organza leaves are tucked between them. When seen through the mist of the bride's veil, they resemble a hidden garden. The rose is Venus's flower but it also became a leitmotiv for Galliano. The bride's shoes were designed by Patrick Cox (b.1963), who launched his own label in 1987. Her dress, which was a bold choice, embodies a spirit of youthful adventure, tempered by a romantic sense of occasion.

Ian Cooper (d.1992) and Marcel Aucoin (d.1991), who designed in London under the name Ian & Marcel, also worked independently of mainstream fashion, using craft skills to create unique garments.[27] In 1989 they made a hand-pleated silk wedding dress and coat (pl.130) inspired by the pleated garments of the Spanish-born textile designer Mariano Fortuny (1871–1949) (pl.128). Both dress and coat are immaculately made and the soft, elastic silk clings to the curves of the body. The sleeveless, full-length dress is finished with ivory satin piping around the armholes and V-neckline, and its hem is weighted with tiny ivory-coloured glass beads. The high-waisted coat is made in two parts, with the upper half joined to the lower by beads stitched between the piped edges of the two pieces of fabric. The upper section, cut from one piece of material, flows over the shoulders and fans out over the upper arm. The coat, which is suggestive rather than revealing, falls to the ground in a pool of fabric.

The designers also created a unique oval-shaped silk net veil, whose edges and centre are decorated with roses drawn in white silicone rubber. The circle of roses which decorates the central area forms a wreath around the bride's head. The outfit is elegant, romantic and sensual and uses impressive craftsmanship to merge tradition and innovation. Although this custom-made outfit was very expensive, its simplicity was the antithesis of the ornate and ostentatious fashions that contributed to the decade's reputation for conspicuous consumption. However it was not an anti-fashion statement. Its wide shoulders and body-hugging form were identifiably from the late 1980s but they interpreted contemporary fashion with soft clinging silk rather than lycra, reflecting the influence of Japanese

thetic to fashion. The work of John Galliano (b.1960) was particularly admired and in 1987 Francesca Oddi (b.1957) commissioned him to make her wedding outfit and dresses for her four bridesmaids (pl.129). Galliano, who had graduated from Saint Martin's School of Art and Design with a first-class degree in 1984, was widely respected for his experimental approach to cut and construction, bold imagination and daring flights of fancy. The bride's outfit consisted of a white organza blouse worn under a cream rayon crêpe-de-chine strapless dress supported by shirred side-panels, with a draped skirt and partial peplum. It was worn with a long-sleeved coat with dropped shoulders, a low-waist seam and skirts draped to create looped curves like those of the dress. The back of the coat and left shoulder are decorated with ivory silk roses, varying in shape from buds to full-blown flowers, which appear to grow against the coat like a rambler rose scrambling over a wall. Other roses made from satin and chiffon

128 Silk satin 'Delphos' dress by Mariano Fortuny, 1910s.

© Fortuny Museum, Venice

130 Pleated silk wedding dress by Ian & Marcel, London, 1989. The net veil is decorated with silicone rubber.

V&A: T.178:1 to 3–1993.

designers like Issey Miyake (b.1938), who offered an alternative, pared-down approach to fashion that many women found attractive.

During the 1970s and 1980s mainstream bridal wear drew on a hotchpotch of historical styles to recreate the 'traditional' white wedding dress. The most popular styles were romantic and feminine, and lace, trained skirts and veils returned to favour. Although some dresses shared features with fashionable evening dress, wedding dresses were full-length and made in shades of white and cream, and their use was limited to the single occasion for which they had been purchased. Yet for women who did not dream of becoming a princess for a day, the conventional white wedding dress was beginning to feel like an uncomfortable cliché.[28]

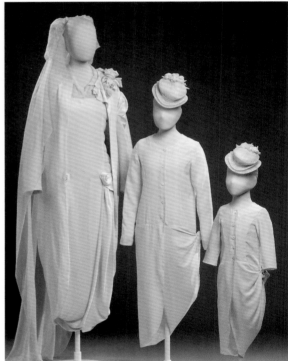

129 Silk and rayon wedding dress, blouse and coat and bridesmaids' dresses by John Galliano, London, 1987. Shirley Hex made the bridesmaids' hats.

V&A: T.41 to D, 42 to B, 43&A–1988. Given by Mrs Francesca Oddi

A civil wedding

On 23 April 1971, when Sara Donaldson-Hudson (b.1948) married Nicholas Haydon (b.1934) at Caxton Hall, the City of Westminster registry office in London, her husband was one of the 1001 divorcés to remarry that year.[1] Until the twentieth century, most remarriages involved either a widow or widower, or both, as divorce was difficult and expensive to obtain, and perceived as scandalous. The gradual relaxing of divorce law and its increasing social acceptability in twentieth-century Britain saw divorces increase from 512 in 1900 to 30,878 in 1950 and 74,437 in 1971, followed by steady six-figure divorce statistics per year onwards.[2]

In contrast to the traditions relating to first weddings, the divorced person had few guidelines for a remarriage outfit. As divorce became more commonplace, the question of what to wear increasingly became an issue – and not only for the divorced party. Although Sara Donaldson-Hudson herself had not been married before, her future husband's marital status affected her outfit. Her mother, who took control of the wedding arrangements, forbade her daughter to wear white to marry a divorcé. Instead, Dorothy Donaldson-Hudson, who was very fashion-conscious, guided her daughter towards a cream wool Bellville Sassoon coat (pl.132). It was hand-painted with vibrant Indian-style floral designs and had been featured in full-colour in British *Vogue* a few months earlier.[3] The coat, lined with orange silk, was worn with an orange shift-dress and matching satin boots made by the Chelsea Cobbler. For the ceremony the mother of the bride wore a smart orange ensemble with matching accessories that coordinated perfectly with her daughter's outfit (pl.131).

Bellville Sassoon were known for their original bridal designs, making them an appropriate choice for Sara's outfit. Her coat, designed for the company by Richard Cawley, came from their Indian-inspired couture collection for Winter 1970/71. The collection included garments named 'Karachi', 'Kathmandu' and 'Nepal'.

'Rajputana', the coat chosen for this wedding, was named after a former group of princely states in north-western India. *Women's Wear Daily* reported that 'Rajputana' was one of the most popular styles and had been ordered by a number of aristocratic clients, including Fiona Thyssen and Pamela, Lady Harlech (see p.149).[4] After being made up, the coat was painted by Andrew Whittle, an illustration student at the Royal College of Art, with a harmonious flowers-and-borders design inspired by Indian artefacts in the V&A. Whittle and Cawley went on to collaborate on other beautiful hand-painted garments.

Daniel Milford-Cottam

131 Dorothy and Sara Donaldson-Hudson and Lt.Col. Ralph Davies-Cooke, 23 April 1971.
V&A: Furniture, Textiles and Fashion Archive

132 'Rajputana' wool coat by Bellville Sassoon, London, 1970.
V&A: T.26–2006
Given by David Sassoon

CHOOSING WHITE

1990s to the present

The link between wedding clothes and contemporary fashion was revitalized in the early 1990s. Although white remained fashionable, as in the 1920s and 1930s, it was not the only stylish colour for a wedding dress. By the second decade of the 21st century, the strong demand for bridal wear in a time of global recession encouraged more designers to invest in the sector, increasing areas of consumer choice.

While the aesthetic and commercial influences are similar to those in earlier periods, recent social and technological developments, particularly the internet, have had an impact on wedding fashions. Fashion like almost every other area of consumer culture has been affected by the role the internet plays in global communications, the instant access it offers to news and events, and its retail applications. In particular the internet has offered the public a new way of engaging with celebrities, and the intense media coverage of their weddings has bolstered the demand for bridal designs that draw on celebrity wedding gowns. Celebrity wedding coverage has also benefited the industry by encouraging higher spending on elaborate wedding celebrations. The introduction of civil partnership ceremonies in 2005 opened up a new market for the wedding industry, while raising questions about what couples should wear. Environmentalism too is prompting new ways of designing and making fashion and challenging the concept of the dress for a day.

BRIDAL WEAR IN THE 1990S

In 1990 the American designer Vera Wang (b.1949) founded a company to offer women ready-made and custom-made wedding dresses that fused bridal and contemporary fashion. Wang felt that bridal fashions in the 1980s had become stereotyped and detached from fashion. She recognized that women were leading increasingly independent lives and having postponed marriage until their late twenties or thirties wanted more sophisticated, trend-driven styles that still made them feel like a bride. Wang was the first American bridal wear designer to make an impact in Europe and the success of her business model was a major influence on bridal design in the 1990s.

In Britain, women who wanted a wedding dress that reflected contemporary fashion could look for an off-the-peg designer dress that was suitable for a wedding, buy a well-designed top-of-the-range ready-made bridal dress or commission a custom-made dress. The difference in price between the best-designed ready-made wedding dresses and couture was narrow, encouraging well-to-do brides who wanted an individual gown tailored to their figure and taste to commission a custom-made garment. A ready-made dress could cost over £1000, while a dress from a London couturier started at about £1500.[1]

British couture, though equally well-made, has always been far less expensive than French couture, as the £15,000 to £60,000 paid for a wedding dress designed by Christian Lacroix (b.1951) in 1994 underlines. The actual cost depended on the quantity of embroidery. Weddings have always been an important market for couturiers, regardless of nationality, because dressing the bride usually involves providing pieces for her trousseau, designing outfits for her attendants and clothing some of the guests – orders which might result in further purchases. Bridal wear was particularly important to Christian Lacroix, accounting for 40% of his house's orders, with eighteen dresses commissioned in 1992 and twelve in 1993. Dior received a similar number of orders, but most French houses designed three or four wedding dresses a year, usually for clients from the Middle and Far East and titled Europeans.[2]

Brides-to-be were drawn to Lacroix by his innovative and free-thinking approach to bridal wear and the unabashed relish with which he overlaid colour, texture and ornament on bold silhouettes. In 1993 the designer donated a stunning black and white bridal dress from his Autumn/Winter 1992–3 couture collection to the V&A (pl.133). The ensemble is richly decorated with faux jewels, gold beads, threads and foil, and garlands of multi-coloured silk and chenille flowers. Grace Mirabella, editor-in-chief of American *Vogue* from 1971–88, described Lacroix as a designer 'for the theatre, for the grand stage, and, ultimately, for women who dream of grand spectacle'.[3]

133 Embroidered silk wedding dress (body, corset and skirt) by Christian Lacroix Haute Couture, Paris, Autumn/Winter 1992–3. The dress's name, *Qui a le droit?* ('Who has the right?') explains the design, which questions whether it is appropriate for a contemporary bride to wear a dress associated with purity and chastity.
Photograph by Guy Marineau
V&A: T.241:1 to 16–1993.
Given by Christian Lacroix

134 Lady Helen Windsor and Timothy Taylor, 18 July 1992. Designer Catherine Walker was inspired by architectural features in St George's Chapel, Windsor Castle, where the couple married.
Photograph by Christopher Simon-Sykes. Camera Press

Catherine Walker (1945–2010) was a French-born couturier based in London. She was well-known for the refined but sexy designs and immaculately crafted garments that made her the Princess of Wales's favourite designer. Her discretion and intelligence enabled her to develop successful working relationships with many high-profile clients for whom she created perfectly fitted, appropriate garments in which they felt confident and attractive. In 1992 she designed the dress (pl.134) which Lady Helen Windsor (b.1964) wore for her marriage to Timothy Taylor (b.1963). The wedding took place in St George's Chapel at Windsor Castle on 18 July 1992. In her autobiography the designer described the meticulous planning that went into this prestigious commission: 'We visited St George's Chapel in order to gauge the correct length of the train, studied the Kent tiara Helen would wear, and sampled embroidery variations … Details such as the Gothic curves of the chapel windows and the pattern of diamonds in the tiara were then incorporated into the design.'[4] The architecture of the chapel was reflected in the wedding gown's crisply curved V-neckline and the upward sweep of its short, cuffed sleeves, while the tiara inspired the pearl and diamanté embroidery that framed and formed a pendant to the collar. Made of silk zibeline, the gently flaring dress was cut to emphasize the fluidity of the body. Although the architecture of the sixteenth-century chapel played an important part in Walker's design, the dress was fresh and modern, with no hint of historical revivalism.

Lisa Butcher (b.1971) married the chef Marco Pierre White (b.1961) in the same year, on 15 August 1992. The bride commissioned Bruce Oldfield (b.1950) to make her wedding dress (pl.135). Oldfield had launched his couture business in 1978 and was well-known for designing glamorous evening dresses for high-profile clients who also included the Princess of Wales. Lisa Butcher was a successful 21-year-old model at a time when models were particularly newsworthy and she clearly wanted a fashionable dress that showed off her excellent figure.

The marriage took place at London's most fashionable Roman Catholic church, the Brompton Oratory. While the bride's figure-hugging white crêpe gown had long sleeves and a train, it was revealingly cut with a wide deep neckline, low-scooped back crossed only by the dress's brassiere-style fastening, and cut-away sides. Her husband was horrified by her choice, later remarking: 'It was wrong for the occasion. I think a woman should dress only for the man she is marrying. It was sexy for the world but not for me.'[5] The dress was essentially an evening gown worn with

135 Lisa Butcher and Bruce Oldfield, 15 August 1992. The shocked groom found the dress, designed by Oldfield, 'sexy for the world, but not for me'.
Alpha Press

136 Pink satin wedding dress by Catherine Rayner, London, 1996.
V&A: T.15–1997.
Given by Catherine Rayner

a bridal veil. Its inappropriateness for a wedding high-lights the delicate balance that a designer has to strike to create a dress that is both bridal and fashionable, while respecting his client's wishes. Lisa Butcher's choice laid her open to accusations of exhibitionism and sadly the marriage ended after fifteen weeks. As the bride later said of her second failed marriage, 'I was young, I had my head in a bubble, and I was the main player in my own movie'.[6] Lisa Butcher donated her wedding dress to a charity raffle and it was subse-quently donated to the V&A.[7]

Although Lisa Butcher's dress was too revealing, the most striking development in the 1990s was the acceptance of wedding dresses with bare shoulders, plunging necklines and low backs which were an extension of the body-conscious fashions of the 1980s. Corsets designed as outerwear teamed with skirts, and dresses incorporating laced bodices sim-ulating corsets, were periodically fashionable for evening wear from the late 1980s and into the next decade. Vivienne Westwood (b.1941) had intro-duced corsets as outerwear in her fashion collection for Spring/Summer 1985. The style filtered through into bridal wear in the 1990s. In 1996 the British bridal wear designer Catherine Rayner created a shell-pink duchesse satin dress with a strapless boned bodice which closes at the back with cross-lacing (pl.136). Its slim skirt is decorated at the waist with a large butterfly-bow that extends into a short train, infusing the back of the dress with graceful femininity. Pale pink was a popular colour for brides who preferred not to wear white, but did not want to make a statement by wearing a stronger colour. Vivienne Westwood launched her made-to-measure bridal collection in 1996 and she has made a speciality of bridal dresses featuring bodices inspired by corsetry.

The influence of evening fashions on bridal wear can also be seen in the made-for-television wedding dress (pl.137) that Deborah Milner (b.1964) designed for 'Nicole', the star of a series of popular advertisements which promoted Renault's Clio car. The low-cut, beaded ivory lace sheath dress has del-icate, slender straps which are also beaded and cross at the back. The finale to the series, broadcast in

137 Beaded lace and silk wedding dress and beaded headdress by Deborah Milner, London, 1998 (above and right). The dress featured in the final episode of Renault's Clio advertising campaign starring Estelle Skornik as Nicole.

(above) Richard Young / Rex Features
(right) V&A: T.40:1,2,-2000
Given by Renault UK Ltd

1998 and watched by an estimated twenty-three million British television viewers, was a spoof of the 1967 film *The Graduate*. As Nicole, her father and the groom stood before the priest, Bob, the man she really loved, raced to the balcony of the church and shouted her name just as the groom was sliding the wedding ring over her finger. Like Elaine in *The Graduate*, Nicole ran from the church and she and Bob roared off in the Clio, as she tossed her bouquet to the rejected groom.

Deborah Milner was a graduate of Saint Martin's School of Art and the Royal College of Art, and although the fashion press recognized her creativity and exceptional cutting skills, she found it difficult to earn a living as a designer. She started making wedding dresses when she shared a studio with the milliner Philip Treacy (b.1967) and they became her main source of income.[8] In 1998 she and Treacy made Selina Blow's (b.1966) outfit for the thanksgiving service in Gloucester Cathedral following her marriage to Charles Levinson (b. 1961). Blow, a fashion designer, was a close friend. The bride chose an ivory-coloured fabric designed for church use by the specialist London firm Watts & Co., from which Milner created a simple, tailored coat-dress with a Nehru collar, cut with a dramatic train which the bride described as being like 'Dracula's cloak' (pl.138). Treacy designed an equally bold arc-shaped gold headdress, whose crown rises to a peak over the brow in a shape reminiscent of roofs in Sri Lanka, the home of Selina Blow's maternal family.

SUSTAINABLE WEDDING FASHIONS

As in wartime Britain, when resources were scarce, factors other than fashion began to determine new approaches to bridal wear in the 1990s. A concern for the environment spawned companies such as Hess Naturtextilien, a German mail-order company specializing in sustainable 'natural' clothing. To celebrate their tenth anniversary in 1996, they extended their eco-friendly credentials by devising a wedding dress loan scheme, using not only sustainable materials, but overcoming the wastefulness of the one-time-only wedding dress by recycling their models for several brides.

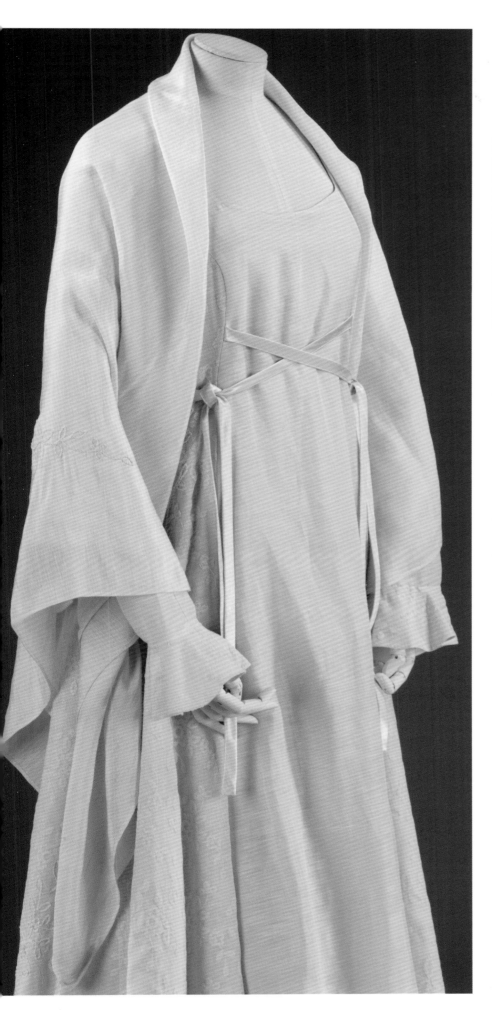

139 Hemp and silk wedding dress and shawl by Veronica Schwandt for the label Hess Natur, Germany, 1996. The hat, made of palm fibre, is trimmed with silk roses.

V&A: T.85:1,2,4–2000.
Given by Hess Naturtextilien GmbH

Their designer, Veronica Schwandt, was asked to create a romantic and timelessly elegant dress that was comfortable and appropriate for women of different shapes and sizes. She designed a dress with a square neckline and long sleeves which is ankle-length on a woman of average height (pl.139). Made from a blend of undyed hemp and silk, it is decorated with hand-embroidered flowers on the cuffs, side panels and back, and can be adjusted to size with silk ties at the waist. The durable material was made from pesticide-free hemp in an energy- and water-efficient production method, which excluded chemicals from the finishing process. In 1999 London's Design Museum short-listed the wedding dress for the Design Sense Award for sustainable products that reflect an understanding of the impact of design on the environment. Following the dress's display in London, the V&A acquired it as an example of a garment that responded to contemporary concerns about damage to the environment and depletion of the world's natural resources.

The environment became a mainstream political issue in Britain and recycling began to be encouraged at local and national level. Although many wedding dresses are worn only for a day, they can be recycled. Wedding dress hire services have, of course, been available since the 1940s but Oxfam, who now have a small chain of bridal shops, only started selling bridal wear in 1960. Today there is an increasing number of retailers who sell once-worn 'pre-loved' dresses. Wedding dresses are also sold on eBay, the online auction and shopping website founded in 1995. Vintage dresses, which are unique and eco-friendly, are a fashionable choice in several senses and designers specialize in cleaning, reconditioning and restyling them for weddings (pl.141).

THE WORLD'S BEST-SELLING BRIDAL MAGAZINE

BRIDES

JULY/AUGUST 2000 £3.80

Great ideas with
wedding flowers

New looks for hair

Real-life brides
lead the way

YOUR DREAM WEDDING STARTS HERE

EQUAL PARTNERS
How to achieve
a balanced marriage

DRESSES • GIFT LISTS • RECEPTIONS • HONEYMOONS • BEAUTY

THE WORLD'S BEST-SELLING BRIDAL MAGAZINE

BRIDES

MARCH/APRIL 2000 £3.80

THE VERY BEST MODERN WEDDING FASHION

LINGERIE HE'LL
LOVE YOU IN

WHAT KIND OF
BRIDE ARE YOU?

GET CHIC:
great outfits for the
mother of the bride

**FREE: REAL-LIFE WEDDINGS
SUPPLEMENT: REAL BRIDES,
REAL IDEAS, REAL STYLE**

THE WORLD'S SEXIEST
BEACH HONEYMOONS

THE MAGAZINE FOR BRIDES WITH STYLE

WEDDING DAY

THE MONTHLY *magazine* FOR BRIDES

FEBRUARY ISSUE £3.00

FASHION EXTRA
Size 14-plus
and
fabulous

The 50
best ever
wedding tips

THE BIG DAY
In Scotland
Staffordshire
Hampshire
Surrey

One bride's
perfect wedding
for £5,000

WIN
■ Jasper Conran
wedding dresses
■ A honeymoon
in Thailand

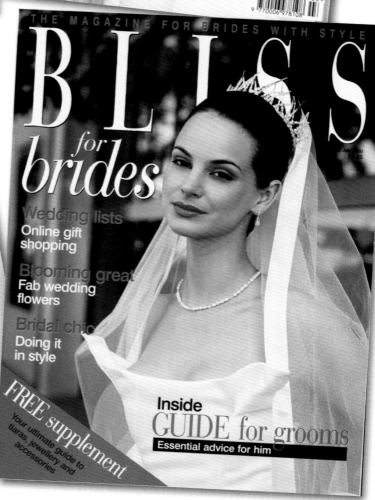

THE MAGAZINE FOR BRIDES WITH STYLE

BLISS
for brides

Wedding lists
Online gift
shopping

Blooming great
Fab wedding
flowers

Bridal chic
Doing it
in style

FREE supplement
Your ultimate guide to
tiaras, jewellery and
accessories

Inside
GUIDE for grooms
Essential advice for him

THE INTERNET AND BRIDAL MAGAZINES

The web became available to the general public in 1993. Since then, it has revolutionized the speed and range of global communication. Retailers were quick to see the medium's potential but the slump in the share value of e-commerce companies trading online ('dot-com' companies) in 2000 sent many companies into liquidation. Others survived the market correction and continued to grow. The turn of the millennium also saw the founding of several online fashion companies which became very successful including ASOS, Figleaves and Net-A-Porter. Figleaves introduced pages selling lingerie for brides in September 2002 and Net-A-Porter launched a wedding boutique in spring 2010, having tested the market by successfully selling wedding dresses within its main offering. The internet was particularly useful to companies selling services and it attracted a growing number of online retailers offering comprehensive guides to wedding planning and links to businesses. Services included practical aids such as wedding planner software, advice on etiquette and speechwriting, the opportunity to download and compare wedding music, and more personalized support such as monthly e-mail updates to keep planning on track.[9]

Specialist wedding magazines remained important to the wedding industry. During the 1980s and 1990s many new titles were launched, including *You and Your Wedding* (1985), *Bride and Groom* (1994), *Martha Stewart Weddings* (1995), *Bliss* (1997) and *Wedding Day* (1999). Although some, like *Martha Stewart Weddings*, were American publications, they were also sold in Britain. They were supplemented by numerous regional wedding magazines, covering local weddings and wedding suppliers. These magazines regularly featured high-profile weddings while advising brides-to-be on how to plan their own. The public's interest in celebrity weddings, and the gossip surrounding them, was fuelled by a raft of celebrity lifestyle magazines which vied with each other to buy the rights to cover weddings. Rivalry in the UK between *Hello!* and *OK!*, launched in 1988 and 1993 respectively, pushed up the fees that couples could earn by offering access to their 'special day'.

CELEBRITY WEDDINGS

In 1999 *OK!* is said to have paid up to £1 million for exclusive world coverage of the wedding of Victoria Adams (b.1974), a member of the British girl band the Spice Girls, and David Beckham (b.1975), the Manchester United and England footballer. The fee enabled the magazine to publish over three successive issues lavishly illustrated interviews with the couple and descriptions of every aspect of the wedding and reception. The event, which took place at Luttrellstown Castle in the Republic of Ireland on 4 July 1999, set new standards in extravagance and stage management. The bride, who already had one child with her husband-to-be, deliberately avoided a sexy dress, stating that she wanted 'to look quite virginal on [her] wedding day'.[10] She chose a champagne-coloured satin dress with a fitted corset-style bodice and full skirt designed by Vera Wang. She liked the dress because it reminded her of Scarlett O'Hara's costumes in the classic 1939 film *Gone with the Wind*, a gripping love story set during the American

142 Wedding dress by Jean Paul
Gaultier, Spring/Summer 2001.
The presence of a baby wrapped
in the bridal veil highlights the
discrepancy between a white
wedding dress's traditional
association with chastity and
social realities today.
Courtesy of Jean-Bernard Villareal / Style.com

**143 Gwen Stefani
and Gavin Rossdale**,
14 September 2002.
Photograph: Thomas Rabsch /
Wire Image

Civil War (1861–5). Instead of a veil, the bride wore
a diamond and gold coronet designed by the jeweller
Slim Barrett (b.1961) and she carried a bouquet of ivy,
brambles, poppyheads, apples and berries which
echoed floral displays in the castle. Her two infant
bridesmaids were dressed as flower fairies.

The London tailor Timothy Everest (b.1961),
who had trained with Tommy Nutter, dressed the
bridegroom in a cream suit with a frock coat and
cream and gold striped waistcoat. Beckham accessorized it with a cream top hat, cream shoes
designed by Manolo Blahnik (b.1942) and a Cartier
diamond bracelet which was a gift from the bride.
Baby Brooklyn, who was in his father's arms when
his mother arrived for the wedding service, was also
in cream, in an ensemble created by the British
designer Antonio Berardi (b.1968). Babes-in-arms
and children were to become increasingly common
at church weddings as couples married after having
children. For the finale to his Spring/Summer 2001
couture collection, French designer Jean Paul
Gaultier (b.1952) sent his 'bride' down the runway
carrying a nappy-clad baby partially wrapped in her
voluminous veil (pl.142). Her appearance evoked
images of the Virgin Mary, while drawing attention
to the discrepancy between social reality and the traditional association of the white wedding dress with
chastity.[11] Fashion designers often use the design of
the wedding dress, which traditionally forms the
finale to the runway show, to make a comment about
contemporary society.

The John Galliano for Dior dress chosen by
Gwen Stefani (b.1969) for her marriage to Gavin
Rossdale (b.1967) on 14 September 2002 was an
unconventional choice for a bride, but accorded with
the singer's interest in fashion. She was to launch her
own fashion line L.A.M.B. in 2003. The bride wore
the dress for her wedding at St Paul's Church in
London's Covent Garden and again, two weeks
later, when she and her husband renewed their vows
in a ceremony in Los Angeles.

The dramatic full-length dress is made of from
lengths of white silk spray-painted bright pink
around the hem with the colour fading away at knee-
height (pl.143). Its cut and construction are

asymmetrical, giving the dress an air of seductive disarray. From the back the bodice appears to have been partially unfastened and pulled away to reveal the lacing of the bride's corset. This imagery is carried through to the front of the bodice where metal corset fastenings are arranged in a slanted line, suggesting that the garment has been yanked out of place. The trained skirt has also been constructed to appear as if it has been subjected to force, causing the side pocket and drapery to twist to the front. The idea of a bride arriving for her wedding partially undressed transgresses a tradition common to many cultures in which the bride is ritually dressed for her wedding. Stefani completed the outfit with a bridal veil appliquéd with antique lace designed by Galliano. The bridegroom was dressed in a fashionable version of a conventional black wool suit. It was designed by Dior Homme with a single-breasted, fly-fronted jacket accented with black satin stripes on the lapels and sleeve vents. The trousers are also trimmed with stripes of black satin which unusually run down the outside front of the legs. The ceremony was attended by Winston, Rossdale's fourteen-year-old Puli sheepdog, which was garlanded with flowers. Retailers responded to the increasing presence of pets at weddings by using the web to advertise suitably decorated accessories, from collars and ties to coats.

The wedding of the model and burlesque artist Dita Von Teese (b.1972) to the rock musician Marilyn Manson (b.1969) was one of the fashion highlights of 2005. The couple were legally married in a midnight civil service at their home in Los Angeles, which they followed on 3 December 2005 with a second 'full-dress' ceremony and extravagant Gothic-styled party at Gurteen Castle in the Republic of Ireland, where they reaffirmed their wedding vows. The bride chose a dramatic violet-coloured, shot taffeta Vivienne Westwood dress and matching veiled tricorne hat, trimmed with mink pompoms and designed by Stephen Jones (b.1957) (pl.145). The dress's fitted low-cut bodice, extravagant skirts and dazzling colour, which highlighted the bride's pale skin, may have enabled her too to 'unleash her Scarlett O'Hara fantasies', but to

Hamish Bowles, the European editor at large for American *Vogue*, she most resembled 'an exquisite eighteenth-century figure come to life'.[12] The silhouette of the dress, like many of Westwood's garments, reflects historical costume, but its cut, and Westwood's bold handling of the fabric of the skirt, are utterly contemporary.

Around 2005 weddings became significantly more lavish and extravagant. The barrage of information about celebrity weddings contributed to this, but the changing lifestyle of women in the West also played a part. As women realized their professional ambitions and became more successful and target-driven at work, they created comparable personal goals. Marriage and a baby before thirty became a mantra in some circles. Encouraged by the prevalent culture of competitiveness, brides vied with their peer group to create the most flawless, memorable and unique wedding, spending extravagantly to achieve it in the belief that a perfectly organized wedding presaged a perfectly organized future.[13]

144 Satin and lace corset by Mr Pearl (Mark Pullin), Paris, 2005, and lace peignoir by Nina Ricci, Paris, 2005. Made for Dita Von Teese's bridal trousseau.
Private collection

145 Dita Von Teese dancing with designer Christian Louboutin, Gurteen Castle, Ireland, 3 December 2005. Louboutin made the bride's wedding shoes.
Photograph by Robert Fairer.
© Robert Fairer

146 Workers at Majestic Bridal embroider beading samples for bridal wear, Zhongshan, 2008.

Photograph by Corina Gertz.
© Corina Gertz

147 Majestic Bridal, Zhongshan, 2008. The Chinese company manufactures mid- to low-priced ready-to-wear dresses for a global market.

Photograph by Corina Gertz.
© Corina Gertz

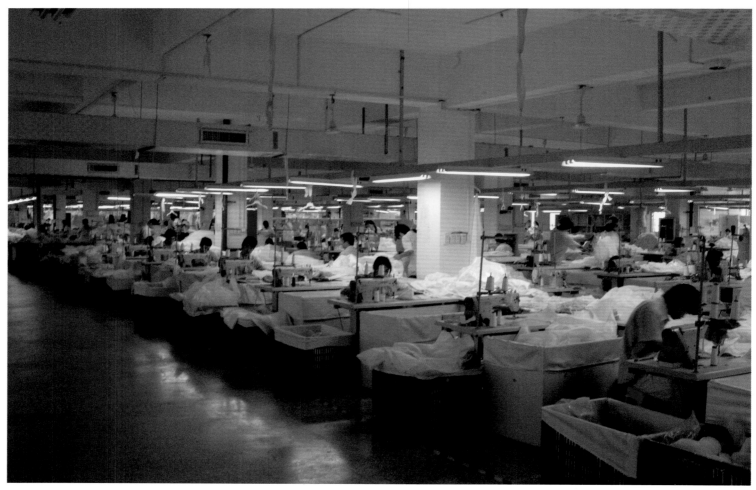

The wedding industry thrived in this time-short, credit-rich environment. In London, the high-fashion boutique Browns expanded to meet the demand. In November 2004 they set up a bridal boutique, Browns Bride, and an associated website, selling wedding garments and accessories from a range of high-end international designers.

Internationalism permeates not just clothing design, but its global manufacture, and the wedding dress industry is no exception. Celebrity culture and world trade, despite their seemingly distinct universes, are interconnected. Most of the mid- to low-priced ready-to-wear wedding dresses sold by bridal wear companies in Britain are now made in China, where celebrity weddings are studied closely by the factories' in-house bridal wear designers. Production in China is less expensive than in Europe and more efficient than in other countries with low labour costs. Chinese factories draw on a huge pool of domestic migrant labour, have modern machinery and access to both home-produced cotton and man-made fibres. Manufacturers are generally reliable and responsive to their customer's needs, though there are growing national and international concerns about working conditions.[14] Many of the companies making bridal wear are Taiwanese-owned. Pretty Fashions, which was founded in 1989 and makes bridal wear as well as other clothing, is among the largest. In 2008 it employed about 6800 people in factories spread over four Chinese provinces. It offers a wider range of quality than most companies and exports wedding dresses to Europe, North and South America, Australia and Africa. Majestic Bridal (pls 146–7), based in Zhongshan in Guangdong Province, manufactures dresses for Europe, North America and Asia. Commissioning companies generally bring their designs to the factory and oversee the choice of fabric, pattern-cutting, construction and decoration of the samples. For their cheaper lines, some companies draw on the factories' own designs produced by their in-house designers and pattern-cutters, and adapt them to the taste of their customers. Using a factory's own range is economical and reduces the risk of production problems.[15]

CIVIL PARTNERSHIP CEREMONIES

The introduction of civil partnership ceremonies in Britain in December 2005, following the enactment of the Civil Partnership Act in 2004, boosted the British wedding industry. The Act offered the opportunity for same-sex couples to enter into a state-sanctioned union. It did not confer the religious associations of marriage through the church, nor some of the tax privileges, but did offer many of the legal rights enjoyed by married couples.

Specialist companies founded in 2004 in anticipation of the ceremonies benefited from the initial rush to register civil partnerships by couples in long-term relationships. Elton John (b.1947) and his partner of ten years David Furnish (b.1962) were among the first to take advantage of the new legal right. Both wore dark morning suits (pl.148), and the publicity they attracted set a pattern for other traditional-style civil partnership ceremonies between men. Matching or harmonised suits in light or bright colours and patterned fabrics also became popular, while more unconventional couples sometimes chose themed costumes. All these ceremonies tend to bear a similarity to the traditional wedding pattern, as the most obvious and visible model, and couples sometimes refer to themselves as married, and talk about their wedding. Couples wishing to have a more low-key ceremony, to mark their relationship or entering into a civil partnership for its resulting legal and financial rights, may choose to wear lounge suits or more casual outfits, reflecting their individual characters.[16] As a

148 Elton John and David Furnish, 21 December 2005. The pair was one of the first celebrity couples to take advantage of new Civil Partnership legislation in the UK.

David Hartley / Rex Features

recent legal development, the ceremony has no set pattern of dress, which gives participants a greater degree of freedom than their heterosexual counterparts. 18,059 civil partnership ceremonies took place in the first year, but by 2007 the number fell by about a half. (There were 273,069 marriages in England and Wales in 2004.)[17]

A morning coat or suit worn for a wedding or civil marriage is not specific to a bridegroom – many male members of the wedding party may be so attired. But a white dress worn in this context is almost invariably suggestive of a heterosexual bride. This poses a dilemma for lesbians entering into a civil partnership who need to find a form of clothing that accords with their sexual identity. Lesbians have resolved this issue in a variety of ways guided by their personality, politics or the sexual dynamics of their relationship. Some women emphasize their femininity and the importance of their public expression of commitment in a traditional way by wearing a white dress (pl.14). Some opt for white trouser suits, which are less commonly worn by brides and visually set the wearer apart from the traditional heterosexual norm. Others make more nuanced or emotional choices. When Amanda Stonham (b.1961) entered into a civil partnership with Catherine Harper (b.1965) on 2 September 2006, she chose a bronze lamé cocktail dress worn by her mother to an aunt's wedding in 1952 (pl.149). It was very important to her to feel her mother's presence during this rite of passage, the experience of which was both similar to and very different from that of her mother. The accumulated memories that adhered to the dress, and its fabric and form, comforted Amanda, who described how she felt 'held in some way'.[18]

A CELTIC BLESSING

The idea of creating one's own wedding ceremony is very much a part of contemporary culture. This is due in part to the secularization of Western society and to the cultural mix of countries like Britain. Cornelia Rudolph (b.1975) wore her mother's bridal headdress of Bohemian crystal stars when she celebrated her marriage to William Sheehy (b.1965) in Killorglin in the Republic of Ireland on 19 July 2008. Her mother was present at her wedding, but they lived at a dis-

tance and the bride did not want to lose touch with her roots. Cornelia Rudolph was born in Thuringia, Germany, and she and her husband-to-be decided to mark the union of their families with a ceremony that incorporated traditions from both their cultures. Following their marriage at a registry office, they received a traditional Celtic blessing with earth, air, fire and water in an ancient stone circle, which marks a sacred site, at Killorglin near the Sheehys' home. A traditional Irish band played music and the groom wore a kilt made by Vivienne Westwood in the Mac Sheehy tartan. Kilts have become a Westwood classic, which the designer enjoys as a glamorous alternative form of male dress made from a traditional fabric. Following a Thuringian custom, the bride's parents made a garland for the couple, incorporating their initials and decorated with green and white ribbons, which was placed on an archway at the entrance to the circle. In Thuringia this would be attached to two pines set up outside the bride's family house.

149 Amanda Stonham and Catherine Harper, 2 September 2006. Amanda Stonham (left) wore her mother's bronze cocktail dress to the couple's civil partnership ceremony at Brighton & Hove Register Office.

Photograph © Michela Mantegazza

150 Cornelia and William Sheehy, 19 July 2008. The couple created a ceremony that blended Celtic and German traditions.

Photograph by Brendan Landy.
© Brendan Landy

Cornelia Rudolph worked in London as a pattern-cutter for Vivienne Westwood until her marriage and her fairy-tale dress (pl.150) was created by Steffen Gerling (b.1966), a former colleague. The dress's colours were chosen to complement the heathery, organic colours in William Sheehy's kilt, which reflect the lush Irish countryside, and the swirling drapery, which passes over the shoulder and is caught at the waist to form a short train, evokes the shawl commonly worn in the past by women in Celtic communities. Nina Farnell-Watson (b.1982), who married Edward Tryon (b.1979) on 19 July 2008, was also a Vivienne Westwood customer. She chose Westwood's 'Bird of Paradise' wedding dress (pl.12), which she wore with a ten-metre-long veil covered with Swarovski crystals and held in place by a striking antique lace tiara created by Philip Treacy (pl.152). The tiara, whose shape was suggested by patterns in the lace, is also decorated with crystals which glisten like dew drops.

BRIDAL WEAR AND GLOBAL RECESSION

In May 2008 when *Sex and the City: the Movie* premiered in London, the world was teetering on the edge of financial crisis. Uninhibited spending on fashion played a significant role in the film's plot, which featured over 300 costume changes. The recently engaged Carrie (Sarah Jessica Parker) models a series of wedding gowns from recent collections by Vera Wang, Carolina Herrera, Christian Lacroix, Lanvin, Dior, Oscar de la Renta and Vivienne Westwood for a *Vogue* fashion shoot. Carrie falls in love with the Westwood dress which is 'so special it would bring a wedding tear from even the most unbelieving of women'. She is subsequently given a slightly different dress by Westwood (pl.151) for her own wedding, to which the groom fails to turn up.

The film prompted a lively discussion on the internet about the merits of the different dresses, giving their designers huge free publicity. The Lanvin dress, designed by Alber Elbaz (b.1961), was a short, flirty mini-dress (pl.153). Most wedding dress collections now include one or two short dresses as weddings take place in such a variety of locations. In spite of the bride's ill-omened rejection, the Westwood wedding dress spawned many copies and in spring 2009 Vivienne Westwood produced a limited edition of another version for Net-A-Porter, retailing at £4,530, which sold out in a day. The success of this collaboration demonstrated that it was possible to sell expensive bridal wear online, even in a harsh economic climate.

The global recession, which followed the banking crisis of August 2008, has affected the bridal industry in different ways. In January 2009, British Home Stores (BHS), the mass-market retailer, cut its prices, offering a simple white bridal outfit with shoes for £100. This reflected its customers' reduced budgets and offered a stark contrast to the £495 dresses designed by Elizabeth Emanuel which it had advertised the previous February.[19] On the other hand, designers at the top end of the market claimed to be benefiting from the continuing demand for well-designed and well-made bridal wear from the well-off, who were determined not to compromise on their wedding dress. This encouraged a number

151 *Sex and the City: the Movie*, 2008. The Vivienne Westwood wedding dress worn by Carrie Bradshaw (Sarah Jessica Parker) in this globally successful film spawned many copies.
© New Line / Everett / Rex Features

of designers including Lanvin, Giambattista Valli, Marchesa and Alberta Ferretti to enter the bridal market with capsule collections. London's Savile Row tailors are also more overtly staking a claim to the bridal market. Richard James (b.1953) contributed a short film on his firm's approach to dressing the bridegroom for a CD-Rom offered with *Brides* magazine. It emphasized their approachability, personal service and consideration for the bride's choices as well as those of the groom.[20]

In May 2009 the average amount spent on a wedding dress at Browns Bride, which sells high-quality designer dresses, was £6000 and bridal sales at Temperley London, which was founded by the designer Alice Temperley (b.1975) in 2000 and specializes in very feminine embroidered and beaded dresses, were 50% higher than the previous year. In October 2009, the couturier Bruce Oldfield opened a bridal boutique to supplement his ready-to-wear and couture boutique and the following spring, Net-A-Porter successfully launched its online bridal boutique. These spending patterns run counter to overall trends in the fashion industry and support the suggestion, mooted in the recession in the early 1990s, that the bridal industry offers designers some stability in a volatile market.[21] Brides-to-be benefited from far greater choice and from reduced prices, which were driven down by the increasingly competitive market.[22]

In 2010, two hundred years after the fashion media began to promote white as the most fashion-able colour for a bridal gown, many women across the world dream of wearing a white dress for their wedding. In doing so, they willingly become part of a tradition which celebrates romantic love and the fairytale beauty of the bride, while being rooted in the materialistic world of commerce. In spite of widespread scepticism, changing moral attitudes and women's increasing independence, the demand for the traditional white wedding dress remains buoyant.

152 **Antique lace tiara** by Philip Treacy, London, 2008. Worn by Nina Farnell-Watson for her wedding to Edward Tryon.
Private collection

153 Silk wedding dress by
Alber Elbaz for Lanvin, Paris,
Spring 2008. Carrie
Bradshaw (Sarah Jessica
Parker) wears a similar
dress in *Sex and the City: the
Movie*. The scene depicts a
Vogue fashion shoot, and *La
Mode Tribune*, a fashion blog,
commended the dress for
turning the 'ageing Carrie'
into a 'young girl'.

Courtesy of Lanvin

154 Jasper Conran,
Autumn/Winter 2007.

Courtesy of Jasper Conran. Photograph by
Tessa Traeger

Opposite clockwise from top left

155 Chanel Haute Couture,
Spring/Summer 2010.

Courtesy of Anthea Sims

**156 Stéphane Rolland Haute
Couture**, Spring/Summer 2010.

Courtesy of Stéphane Rolland Haute Couture

157 Dior Haute Couture,
Autumn/Winter 2007.

© Camera Press / Mitchell Sams

158 Reem Acra, Autumn/Winter
2010.

Courtesy of Reem Acra

159 Their Royal Highnesses the Prince of Wales and Duchess of Cornwall, 9 April 2005. For the blessing following her marriage to the Prince of Wales, the Duchess of Cornwall chose an outfit designed by Anna Valentine accessorised with a headdress created by Philip Treacy. This photograph, taken in the White Drawing Room at Windsor Castle, shows the couple with their children, Prince Harry, Prince William, Laura and Tom Parker-Bowles.

Photograph by Hugo Burnand / Clarence House / Pool / Getty Images

160 Duke and Duchess of Cambridge, 29 April 2011. To wed Prince William, Catherine Middleton wore a silk gazar dress by British designer Sarah Burton for Alexander McQueen. It was decorated by embroiderers from the Royal School of Needlework with hand-appliquéd motifs in the style of Carrickmacross lace. The bride's ivory silk tulle veil was held in place by a 1936 Cartier tiara lent by Queen Elizabeth.

Photograph by Hugo Burnand / Clarence House / Camera Press

Clockwise from top
161 Bruce Oldfield Couture,
Spring/Summer 2010.
Courtesy of Bruce Oldfield

162 Jenny Packham,
Spring/Summer 2010.
Courtesy of Jenny Packham

163 Marchesa,
Spring/Summer 2010.
Courtesy of Marchesa

164 Temperley London,
'Long Jean Dress', 2010.
Courtesy of Temperley London

Overleaf
165 Ian Stuart, Revolution
Rocks Collection, 2011. This
photo-shoot was inspired by
the film *Marie Antoinette* (2006),
directed by Sophia Coppola and
starring Kirsten Dunst.
Courtesy of Ian Stuart. Photograph
by Iain Philpott

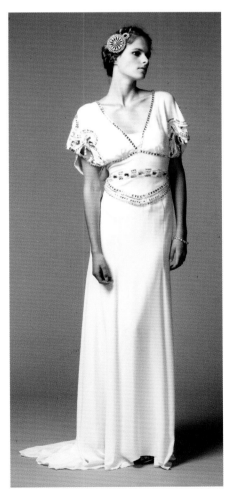

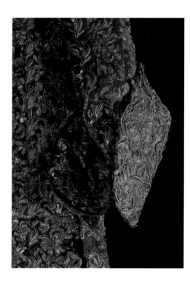

T.711:1-1995

Pre-1800

1673
Coat and breeches. Heather wool embroidered in silver and gold thread.
Worn by James, Duke of York (later James II & VII of England & Scotland) for the confirmation of his marriage to Mary of Modena, at Dover, Kent, on 21 November.
T.711:1, 2-1995

1681
Coat and breeches. White silk brocaded with silver-gilt thread. Reputedly made for the wedding of Sir Thomas Isham on 9 August.
175&A-1900

1740s
Dress. Blue silk damask. Associated with a wedding in the donor's family.
Given by Mrs M.C. Alston.
T.382-1984

1744
Court mantua and petticoat. White silk embroidered in coloured silks and silver thread.
Made for the court presentation in London of the Hon. Isabella Courtenay following her marriage to Dr John Andrew at Exeter Cathedral, Devon, on 14 May.
T.260&A-1969

1745
Waistcoat. Ivory silk satin embroidered in coloured silks and silver thread.
Worn by William Morshead for his marriage to Olympia Treise in Blisland, Bodmin, Cornwall, on 23 April.
T.94-1931

1748
Shoes. Pink silk satin trimmed with braid.
Worn by Mrs E. Growden on 22 January.
Given by the executors of the late Miss Laura M. Bodcock.
T.65&A-1935

1750s
Sack-back gown. Blue silk brocaded with silver thread and trimmed with silver lace. Associated with a wedding in the donor's family.
Given by Miss R. Alder.
T.343-1965

1756
Piece of silk brocade. Coloured flowers on cream ground. British (Spitalfields), woven about 1747. Said to be from a dress worn by Sarah Hubbard to marry Thomas Fayerweather in Cambridge, Massachusetts, USA.
Given by Mrs Eleanor Fayerweather.
T.126-1962

T.94-1931

1775–80
Court dress and petticoat. White silk satin trimmed with fly fringe. Probably made for the court presentation of an unknown bride. Given by the executors of the estate of Miss Mary Gorham.
T.2&A-1947

1779
Dress and petticoat. White silk woven with silver strip and trimmed with silver fringe.
Worn by Sarah Boddicott to marry Samuel Tyssen in Hackney, London, on 28 September.
Given by Mrs R. Stock.
T.80&A-1948

1789
Dress and stomacher. Blue silk woven with cream zigzag stripes and flowers, woven about 1755-60. Inscription inside bodice: 'Jean Smith married 20th April 1789'.
939&A-1902

1800–49

1810
Shoes. White leather.
Worn by Miss E. Brown to marry Mr Grimshaw on 7 February.
Given by Mrs Elgood.
T.193&A-1914

c.1820
Dress. Cream silk trimmed with braid, buttons and muslin frills. Worn by Charlotte Cooley to marry Cyrus Sullivan Clark in Stockbridge, Massachusetts, USA. Given by Mrs Campbell.
T.36-1951

c.1820
Bonnet-veil. Net with Carrickmacross appliqué work. Reputedly worn by Miss Wise to marry Mr Hare of Curtisknowe, South Devon.
Later worn by their daughter Matilda E. Hare to marry the Reverend George Dawson in Woodleigh, South Devon, on 4 June 1844.
Given by Miss Louisa Dawson.
T.40-1945

1820–24
Dress. Ivory figured silk trimmed with padded silk satin.
Given by Miss Amanda C. Dickie.
T.5:1 to 3-2000

1821
Dress. Cream silk trimmed with silk satin with long gauze oversleeves.
Worn by Sophia Donaldson to marry William Artindale in Kingston-upon-Hull, Yorkshire, on 17 December.
Given by the Misses F. & M. Mold.
T.127-1929

c.1823
Dress and jacket. Pale pink figured silk trimmed with pink silk satin. Worn by an unknown bride.
T.288&A-1983

1827
Dress. White cotton trimmed with lace and later whitework insertions.
Worn by Elizabeth Stephens to marry William Rowe in St Agnes, Cornwall, on 20 March.
Given by the executors of the late Mr George Rowe of Bridgwater.
T.4-1916

1828
Short-sleeved dress with long oversleeves and a pelerine for daywear. Striped cream silk trimmed with pale gold silk satin and lace. Headdress of net over a silk satin-covered framework. Worn by Eliza Larken to marry William (later 6th Baron) Monson at St Giles in the Fields Church, Covent Garden, London, on 8 May. Headdress given by Lord Monson and Mrs B.N. Phillips.
T.124:1, 2; 373; 374:1, 2-2009

1828
Dress. White silk crêpe embroidered with silver strip. Embroidered white silk satin garters. Embroidered cream silk shoes. Worn by the Hon. Frances Barrington to marry William Legge, 4th Earl of Dartmouth. Given by the Hon. Mrs Brooke.
T.9 to D-1929

1830–45
Bonnet veil. Cream silk gauze with a floral design.
Worn by an unidentified bride. Later worn by Mary Ford to marry William Cowdie in Gloucester in 1874.
Given by Mrs M.E. May.
T.236-1960

1832
Waistcoat. Maroon silk woven with a floral design.
Worn by the donor's great-great-grandfather.
Given by F.F. Bartlett.
T.101-1963

1833
Pair of gloves. White kid with cream silk satin and lace cuffs.
Worn by an unknown bride on 21 May.
Given by Miss Stephenson.
T.24&A-1935

1834
Pelisse robe. White embroidered muslin over white silk.
Associated with a wedding in the Mayo family, probably that of Herbert Mayo and Mary-Anne-Grace Quin who married at St Mary's Church, Stoke Newington, London, on 3 November.
Given by Miss Gaster.
T.63-1973

c.1840
Handkerchief. White embroidered cotton.
Made by Mary Allam for her marriage to Mr Barthald in London.
Given by Mrs Mordent.
T.222-1973

T.24&A-1935

T.250-1927

1840
Overskirt. Net worked with Carrickmacross appliqué floral motifs.
Worn by Betsy Vivian to marry William Gibson Craig in Swansea, Glamorgan, Wales, in August.
Given by Mrs Onslow Panson.
T.250-1927

Early 1840s
Dress. Ivory embroidered net over silk satin. Silk satin shoes. Carrickmacross appliqué veil.
Shoes made by Hird & Son, 8 Lower Grosvenor Place, Pimlico, London.
Given by the Misses Beale.
T.238 to C-1917

1841
Dress. Cream figured silk satin trimmed with silk, silk satin and net.
Given by Miss H. Bousfield.
T.17-1920

1841
Dress. White cotton block-printed with a coloured abstract design.
Worn by Sarah Maria Wright to marry Daniel Neal at St Nicholas's Church, Skirbeck, Lincolnshire, on 27 July.
Given by Sheila Battram and Linda Graham.
T.27-2006

1843
Short-sleeved dress with wrist-length undersleeves. Red silk satin.
Worn by Agnes Eleanor Hubbersty to marry Nicholas Price Wood in Darley, North Yorkshire, on 27 April.
Given by Miss W.D. Wood.
T.30 to C-1945

1844
Waistcoat. Black velvet with red, yellow and blue tartan design.
Worn by William Bingham to marry Mary Louisa Whitehead in Hampstead, London.
Given by Irene Bingham Taylor.
T.62-1970

1845
Waistcoat. White and silver figured silk.
Worn by John Montefiore to marry Julia Norman in London on 28 January.
Given by the Misses Montefiore.
T.668-1919

1845
Bonnet. Cream silk tulle, crêpe and silk satin, trimmed with orange-blossom.
Worn by the donor's mother.
Given by Miss H. Blanche Buckley.
T.69-1929

1848
Shirt. Embroidered cotton.
Worn by Mr Eeles.
Given by Francis C. Eeles.
T.561-1919

1848
Waistcoat. Ivory silk satin embroidered with lily of the valley and forget-me-nots.
Worn by Mr Eeles.
Given by Francis C. Eeles.
T.562-1919

1848
Dress. White silk satin overlaid with embroidered net. White silk satin bonnet. Handkerchief of bobbin lace and embroidered lawn. Embroidered garters.
Worn by Henrietta Woodcock to marry John Bell in Manchester Cathedral, Lancashire, on 28 June.
Given by the daughters of the late Mrs John Bell.
T.53 to E, J-1930

T.69-1929

1848
Waistcoat. White figured silk.
Worn by Joseph Benson Woolmer to marry Mary Hannah Chester in Chesterfield, Derbyshire, on 12 October.
Given by Mrs E. A. Woolmer.
T.182-1927

1848
Dress. Cream silk satin overlaid with embroidered muslin and trimmed with Valenciennes lace. Cream silk satin bag.
Worn by Mary Hannah Chester to marry Joseph Benson Woolmer in Chesterfield, Derbyshire, on 12 October.
Given by Mrs E. A. Woolmer.
T.180 to C-1927

1848
Fragment of a shirt. White cotton embroidered with acorns and oak leaves.
Worn by Edward Morley Perkins to marry Octavia Shuter in Coulsdon, Surrey, on 9 November.
Given by Mrs Herbert Terry.
T.147-1925

1850–99

c.1850
Shawl. Lace made in Bedfordshire in the Maltese style.
Worn by a widow to marry William Price Jones in Bala, Gwynedd, Wales.
Given by Mrs L. Cartledge.
T.81-1964

1851
Dress. White muslin. Straw bonnet trimmed with lace.
Worn by Eliza Sneath to marry Joseph Candlin in Sheffield.
Given by Mrs Bessie Miller.
T.366, 367-1988

1851
Dress. Cream moiré silk trimmed with fringe. Silk satin shoes. 'Norma' wreath of artificial orange-blossom. Cream moiré silk parasol with ivory handle.
Worn by the bride of Major Mackay-Mackenzie on 15 September.
Given by the family of the late Major and Mrs Mackay-Mackenzie.
T.203 to F-1915

1853
Waistcoat. White silk figured with green floral sprigs.
Worn by George Higgs to marry Ann Smith Corderoy at the Brunswick Wesleyan Chapel, Dorset Square, London, on 12 July.
Given by Miss C.M. Higgs.
T.121-1949

T.37-1951

1854
Wreath. Tinted feathers and silk ribbon.
Worn by Elizabeth Wroughton Richards to marry the Reverend Andrew Nugée in Farlington, Hampshire, on 8 August.
Given by Edward Nugée QC.
T.6-2008

1854
Shoes. Cream silk satin.
Made by Chapelle, Paris.
Worn by Elizabeth Wroughton Richards to marry the Reverend Andrew Nugée in Farlington, Hampshire, on 8 August.
Given by Edward Nugée QC.
T.4:1, 2-2008

1855
Wedding veil. Tambour-embroidered net.
Worn by Eliza Smith to marry Adolphus W. Dixey in St Pancras, London.
Given by Miss Trevelyan.
T.292-1973

1856
Dress. Blue-purple shot silk with gilt buttons.
Worn by Jemima Margaret Jay to marry George Francis York at the Parish Church of St George, Bloomsbury, Middlesex.
Given by Miss J.M. Lunnon.
T.210-1998

1856
Dress. White muslin. White silk bonnet. Cream kid shoes.
Worn by Jane Harman Manclark to marry Albert Buck in Medway, Kent, on 30 April.
Given by Mrs A.B. Skottowe.
T.247 to 249-1965

1856–60
Dress. White silk trimmed with silk fringe.
Given by Lady Osborn.
T.119&A-1953

1857
Petticoat. Embroidered cambric.
Made and worn by Ann Cross Price to marry Mr Tucker on 31 October.
Given by Miss A.G. Tucker.
T.177-1931

1857
Dress. Ivory silk. Wax orange-blossom wreath.
Worn by Margaret Scott Lang to marry Henry Scott at the Marylebone Presbyterian Church, London.
Given by the Misses I. & N. Turner.
T.10 to C-1970

1858
Shirt. White embroidered cotton.
Worn by John Stavordi in Marseilles, France.
Given by Mrs Margaret Stavordi.
T.334-1970

1858
Waistcoat. Cream figured silk.
Retailed by Walter Ray Jones, London.
Worn by George Knight to marry Elizabeth Gurr in Kent.
T.313:1-2009

1859
Dress. Blue striped silk trimmed with black lace and beads.
Made by James Spence, St Paul's Churchyard, London.
Worn by the donor's mother.
Given by Mrs Myatt.
T.163&A-1929

1850s
Wedding veil. Needle and bobbin lace.
Given by Mrs R. Marchand and Mrs Aronson.
T.739-1974

c.1860
Wedding veil. Honiton lace.
Given by HM Queen Mary.
T.233-1959

1860
Dress. Pale gold figured silk trimmed with chenille braid and fringe.
Worn by Elizabeth Manks to marry Alfred Oakley Pollard in Elland, Yorkshire, on 9 January.
Given by Mrs H.P. Statham.
T.190&A-1964

1862
Dress. White silk trimmed with ruching and lace.
Worn by Eliza King to marry John Oakey in Brixton Hill, London, on 30 October.
Given by Mrs F. Nelson-Smith.
T.12 to F-1979

1864
Corset. Blue silk.
Associated with a wedding in the donors' family.
Given by the Burrows family.
T.169-1961

1865
Dress. White silk satin and Honiton lace. Honiton lace veil. White kid ankle boots.
Worn by Eliza Penelope Clay to marry Joseph Bright at St James's Church, Piccadilly, London, on 16 February.
Bequeathed by Miss H.G. Bright.
T.43 to C-1947

1867
Dress. White silk satin trimmed with lace.
Worn by Charlotte Clark to marry James Fowler Dwight in Stockport, Massachusetts, USA, on 3 October.
Given by Mrs Campbell.
T.37-1951

1869
Dress. White silk satin trimmed with tulle and orange-blossom.
Worn by Anne-Katharine Mayo to marry Peter Bayne at St John's, Hampstead, London, on 17 February.
Given by Miss Gaster
T.64 to B-1973

1870
Dress. Bright purple silk trimmed with lace. White kid ankle boots with purple silk-covered heels.
Worn by the donor's mother.
Given by Leonard Shields.
T.182&A,183&A-1914

1870
Dress. Purple-blue shot silk with later black braid and lace trimming.
Worn by Mary Anne Bennett to

T.182&A-1914

T.47-1947

marry Joseph Edward Bardwell at St Mary's Church, Stratford-at-Bow, London, on 22 December.
Given by Mrs May Parsons.
T.256&A-1979

1871
Necktie. Blue silk satin, ready-tied in Windsor knot.
Worn by Major D.C. Courtney in Malta.
Given by Dame Kathleen Courtney.
T.194-1964

1871
Frock coat. Black wool.
Worn by Robert O'Brien Furlong in Dublin, Ireland, on 29 June.
Given by Mr A.W. Furlong.
T.47-1947

1872
Dress. White silk trimmed with cream silk satin.
Worn by the donors' mother.
Given by Mr C.F. Hopley and Miss Muriel Hopley.
T.86 to C-1923

1872–4
Dress. Cream silk satin trimmed with tulle and Honiton lace.
Made by E. Gill, 93 New Bond Street, London.
Given by Mrs W.M. Sivewright.
T.390 to B-1980

1873
Flounce. Brussels lace.
Worn by the donor's mother in April.
Later worn by the donor to marry Major Charles Burnett on 6 August 1903.
Bequest of Mrs Violet Georgina Burnett.
T.109-1969

1874
Dress and mantle. Cream striped silk gauze trimmed with cream machine-made lace.
Worn by Lucretia Crouch to marry Benjamin Seebohm at the Friends' Meeting House, Clevedon, on 10 September.
Given by Miss Felicity Ashbee.
T.68 to D-1962

1874
Dress. Grey-blue moiré silk trimmed with silk satin and brown wool lace.
Said to have been a widow's second-wedding dress.
Given by Miss G.D. Delano.
T.166&A-1962

1874
Dress. White striped silk-wool blend trimmed with muslin, silk satin and crochet.
Made by Cowper & Co., 13 St Anne's Square, Manchester.
Worn by Lizzie Lord.
Given by Miss W.P.H. Masters.
T.78 to C-1962

c.1875
Wedding veil. Brussels and bobbin needle-lace on net.
Bequeathed by Miss A.C. Innes.
T.340-1972

1876–7
Dress. Ivory figured silk trimmed with tulle and silk satin.
Made by Mrs Heron, Southampton.
Given by the London Academy of Music and Dramatic Art.
T.89 to B-1959

1877
Handkerchief. Embroidered cotton lawn edged with Honiton lace.
Carried by Grace May to marry Henry John Lawrence on 30 May.
Given by Miss M.S. Lawrence.
T.265-1979

T.62C, D-1976

T.92&A-1949

1878–80
Dress. Brown silk taffeta with smocked panels.
Worn by the bride of Sir John Robinson.
Given by Captain F. Whitworth QC.
T.521&A-1974

1879
Dress. Dark purple-black silk satin with beading and chenille fringe.
Worn by Mrs Elizabeth Smith for her wedding at St John's Church, Clapham, London.
Given by Mrs A. Nicholls.
T.113-1964

c.1880
Waistcoat. Black silk brocaded with white and brown scrollwork and pink and blue flowers.
Worn by George Bowden to marry Martha in Glossop, Derbyshire.
Bequeathed by Miss E.J. Bowden
T.249-1968

c.1880
Dress. White ribbed silk.
Made by Mrs Francis of Great Portland Street, London.
Given by the Reverend W.H. Padget.
CIRC.203-1958

1880
Dress. Ivory silk satin with pearl beading. White silk satin ankle boots. Cream velvet train.
Designed by Charles Frederick Worth of Paris.
Worn by Clara Mathews to marry Colonel Hugh Stafford, at St George's Church, Hanover Square, London, on 19 February.
Given by Mrs G.T. Morton.
T.62 to D-1976

c.1880
Bonnet. Pale blue silk satin trimmed with white lilac and ivy.
Given by Miss Juliet Reckitt and Messrs G.F & A.L. Reckitt.
T.164-1923

c.1882
Dress. Cream ruched silk satin. Silk satin shoes. Embroidered cotton handkerchief. Swansdown fan. Silk net veil.
Made by Harris J. Toms, Costumiers, 4 Princes Street, Cavendish Square, London.
Given by Mrs G.M. Worrall.
T.1 to H-1958

1883
Wedding veil. Brussels application lace on net.
Given by Miss Viola M. Cooper.
T.198-1957

1883
Dress. White silk satin trimmed with lace, ribbons and orange-blossom.
Made by the Misses Nimmo, 107 Portland Street, London.
Given anonymously.
T.45 to B-1947

1883
Dress. Cream silk damask and silk satin trimmed with lace, ribbon and orange-blossom.
Made by Hannington & Sons, Brighton.
Worn by Elizabeth, the bride of Mr C.J. Adams, in Brighton in October.
Given by Mrs C.J. Adams.
T.220-1917

1885
Dress. Cream silk satin trimmed with embroidered net and pearls. Cream silk shoes. Silk stockings. Net veil.
Made by Gladman & Womack, 26 Portman Street, London.
Worn by May Primrose to marry Major Herbert Littledale at St Philip and St James Church, Cheltenham, Gloucestershire, on 10 June.
Given by the Hon. Mrs S.F. Tyser.
T.428 to I-1990

1886
Shoes. Cream silk satin with beading.
T.92&A-1949

1886
Handkerchief. Embroidered muslin edged with Honiton lace.
Carried by Mary Sinkins Clark to marry Charles E. Howlett at the Church of St Mary, Wingfield, Trowbridge, Wiltshire, on 23 September.
Given by Miss Muriel N. Hall.
T.233-1963

1887
Shoes. White silk satin.
Worn by Edith Isabel Alston to marry Francis Edward Nugée in Oundle, Northamptonshire.
Given by Edward Nugée QC.
T.5:1, 2-2008

1887
Corset. White silk satin.
Made by Edwin Izod.
Worn by the donor's mother.
Given by Miss Benjamin.
T.265&A-1960

1888
Dress and mantle. Bronze corded silk trimmed with striped silk, lace and beads.
Worn by Letitia Basnet to marry Joseph Thomas at St Chad's Chapel, Tushingham, Cheshire, on 24 May.
Given by Mrs D. Weller.
T.308 to B-1982

1889
Dress. Cream silk satin, velvet and lace. Wreath of orange-blossom and myrtle.
Worn by Ella Alston to marry Mr Lewin in Bromley, Kent.
Given by Mrs V.I. Lewin.
T.265 to B, 266-1971

T.265&A-1960

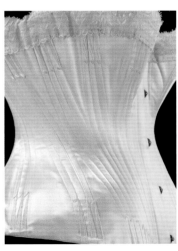

1889
Dress. White silk satin and silk brocade. Silk satin shoes. Orange-blossom wreath.
Worn by the donor's mother.
Given by the Comtesse de Tremereuc.
T.365 to D-1960

Late 19th century
Wedding veil. Honiton lace.
Bequeathed by Mrs S.B.P. Lawrie.
T.15-1963

1890
Piece of embroidered net lace.
Part of the donor's mother's wedding dress.
Given by Mrs R. Rubens.
T.157-1964

1890
Dress. Cream corded silk decorated with silk crêpe, pearls, paste gems, and velvet appliqués. Beaded silk shoes. Silk stockings. Dress made by Stern Brothers, New York. Worn by Cara Leland Huttleston Rogers to marry Bradford Ferris Duff in New York, on 17 November.
Given by Major and Mrs Broughton.
T.276 to F-1972

1892
Wedding cap and veil. Brussels point-de-gaze needle-lace.
First worn by Roxana Atwater Wentworth to marry Clarence Winthrop Bowen in the USA on 28 January.
Later worn by her daughter Roxana Wentworth Bowen in 1917. Also worn by an unknown bride in the mid-20th century.
T.366, 367-1970

1892
Dress. White grosgrain and silk satin trimmed with pearls, chiffon and embroidered net.
Worn by Mary Fox to marry Harold Deans in St Pancras, London, on 29 September.
Given by Miss W.M. Deans.
T.259 to D-1958

1894
Dress. Grey silk satin trimmed with heavy cream lace.
Made by Peter Robinson, London. Worn by Miss Flattelby to marry Mr Kingah in Pimlico, London, in August.
Given by Miss J. Spy.
T.44&A-1958

1894
Dress. White silk satin trimmed with embroidered crêpe chiffon.
Given by Mrs G. Squires.
T.896:1, 2-1994

1896
Dress. White figured silk satin and crêpe chiffon.
Worn by the donor's mother on 13 January.
Given by Mrs Weekley.
T.22&A-1966

1898
Dress. Ivory silk satin and chiffon beaded with pastes and pearls.
Made by Russell & Allen, London. Worn by Miss Gordon to marry Mr Lawson Johnston at the Church of St John the Evangelist, Stanmore, Middlesex, in September.
Given by the Hon. Hugh Lawson Johnston.
T.93&A-1959

1899
Dress. Purple silk grosgrain trimmed with cream silk satin, lace and braid.
Made and worn by Harriett Joyce to marry Percy Raven Sams in South Wimbledon, London, on 8 June.
Given by Mrs Muriel Baker.
T.309&A-1982

1900–20

1900
Dress. Cream silk satin, muslin and lace trimmed with pearls.
Made by W. Mulhall, New York. Worn by Charlotte Mabel Dwight to marry Charles Edmund Akers at St Paul's Church, Stockbridge, Massachusetts, USA on 26 April.
Given by Mrs Campbell.
T.38 to B-1951

1902
Dress. Silk organza over silk satin, decorated with hand-painted and embroidered designs.
Designed by Sarah Fullerton Monteith Young.
Worn by the Hon. Alice Sibell Grosvenor to marry the Hon. Ivor

T.100B, C-1933

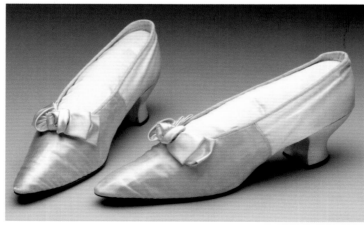

Churchill Guest MP at St Peter's Church, Eaton Square, London, on 10 February.
Given by Viscount Wimborne.
T.215 to C-1976

1902
Dress. Cream silk. Headdress of orange-blossom.
Made by Houghton & Dalton, 10 Church Road, Upper Norwood. Worn by Edith Constance Jardine Hope Murray to marry Mr T.H. Senior in London on 18 June.
Given by Mrs Joyce Pepler in memory of her mother Mrs Edith Senior.
T.260 to C-1990

1903
Dress. Cream silk satin trimmed with chiffon. Silk satin shoes.
Worn by Agnes Madeline Pattisson to marry Martin Hardie in Tunbridge, Kent.
Given by Mrs Martin Hardie.
T.100 to C-1933

1904
Dress. White poplin trimmed with gauze and crochet.
Worn by the donor's mother.
Given by Charles A. Ryder.
T.605&A-1974

1905
Corset. White silk satin trimmed with lace and orange-blossom.
Worn by Marie, the bride of Mr G.E. Dixon.
Given by Mrs G.E. Dixon.
T.90-1928

1907
Dress. Cream silk satin trimmed with lace and ball fringe.
Worn by Annie Beatrice Lindsay to marry Robert McKie at All Saint's Church, Grosvenor Square, Manchester, on 10 June.
Given by Miss McKie.
T.335:1, 2-1992

T.52-1957

c.1907–8
Dress and train. White silk satin embroidered with seed pearls. Lace sleeves and chemisette.
Designed by Liberty & Co, London.
Given by Mr Stewart Liberty.
T.463 to B-1976

1908
Dress. Cream silk and lace.
Designed by Fanny Setti, Italy. Worn by Stuarta Frances Yates Brown-Weyerman to marry Arthur Burton Buckley in Albara, Genoa, Italy, in July.
Given by Rosemary Buckley.
T.779:1, 2-1995

1908
Dress. Ivory silk satin overlaid with net, trimmed with silk piping and fringe.
Designed by Madame Meynier of Lille, France.
Worn by Elaine Campbell Wakefield to marry Claude Llewellyn Thornley Phillips at St George's, Hanover Square, London, on 27 July.
Given by Mrs D.C. Mason.
T.288&A-1971

1909
Dress. Warp-printed flowered silk trimmed with heavy furnishing lace.
Worn by Helen Pearl Humphry to marry George Jefferys Adam at St George's, Hanover Square, London.
Given by the friends of the late Pearl Adam.
T.52-1957

1910
Dress. Cream silk and chiffon with blue silk waistband.
Designed by Madame Paquin, Paris.
Worn by Hedwig Ann Plischke to marry Frederick Charles French in

Kingston, Surrey, in September. Given in memory of Mrs H.A.E.F. Brookes.
T.341:1 to 3-1992

1910
Dress. Cream silk satin trimmed with embroidered net and chiffon. Designed by Nancy Norman, 19 Bessborough Gardens, London. Given by Mrs J. Walford.
T.85-1965

1910
Dress. White silk and wool blend, trimmed with lace and ball fringe. Worn by Louisa Catherine Wittmann to marry Frederick Charles Linton at St Andrew's Parish Church, Bethnal Green, London, on 23 July. Given by Miss I.K. Linton.
T.374&A-1970

1911
Dress. White silk satin trimmed with lace, muslin and fringe. Silk satin shoes. Given by Miss Olive Matthews.
T.39 to B-1946; T.3&A-1947

1911
Dress. Cream silk draped with beaded lace and net. Worn by Lady Dorothy Edith Isabel Hobart-Hampden to marry the Hon. Claude Hope-Morley at the Parish Church of Hampden, Buckinghamshire, on 6 July. Given by the family of Lady Dorothy Hope-Morley.
T.154-1973

1913
Dress adapted to wear at court. Gold-brocaded silk gauze over cream silk satin trimmed with bobbin lace. Cream silk satin court train trimmed with tulle and gold lamé. Silk satin shoes. Silk stockings. Designed by Reville & Rossiter Ltd, 15 &16 Hanover Square, London. Worn by Cicely Hilda Farmer to marry Henry Warrington Smyth Baden-Powell at All Saints Church, Knightsbridge, London, on 13 September. Subsequently worn to court, May 1914. Worn and given by Mrs C.H. Baden-Powell.
T.109 to H-1927

1914
Dress. Ivory silk satin, gauze and lace. Worn by Constance Clervaux Chaytor to marry Godfrey Percy Burrell at St. Luke's Church, Marlboroughtown, New Zealand, on 17 June 1914.

Given by Frances M. Plaisted.
T.260:1 to 11-1992

1914
Dress and train. Ivory silk satin, beaded lace and tulle. Shoes of silver brocade. Dress designed by Aida Woolf, 283 Oxford Street, London. Shoes retailed by Peter Robinson, Oxford Street, London. Worn by Phyllis Blaiberg to marry Bertie Mayer Stone at the Bayswater Synagogue, Chichester Place, London, on 9 September. Given by Mrs B. Rackow.
T.856 to C-1974

1915
Dress. Cream crêpe-de-chine with cream and silver embroidery. Designed and made by Mrs M. and Miss M.A. Grundy. Worn by Eva Minnie Gartell to marry Edgar Bentley Hyde in Oldham, Lancashire, on 5 June. Given by Mrs Barbara Stone.
T.722-1997

1916
Dress. White silk and net. Designed by Violet Tripp. Worn by Grace Allen Nash to marry Sydney O'Connell Finigan at St George's, Hanover Square, London on 8 June. Given by Mrs J. Blair and Mrs D. Street.
T.415-1996

1920s

1922
Dress and train. Cream silk satin trimmed with lace and wax orange-blossom. Cream silk petticoat trimmed with lace, pearls and silver lamé ribbon. Two pink silk garters and a third oyster silk satin garter. Designed by Lucile, London. Worn by Amy Colville to marry Steven Bilsland at St Giles Cathedral, Edinburgh, Scotland, on 16 February. Given by Mrs Norman Colville.
T.314 to F-1985

1923
Dress. Silver lamé and beaded silver lace. Train of silver lamé trimmed with pink silk.

T.314F-1985

Designed by Aida Woolf, 283 Oxford Street, London. Worn by Flora Diamond to marry Phillip Jacobs at the Bayswater Synagogue, Chichester Place, London, in June. Given by Mrs A. Diamond.
T.65&A -1973

1923
Dress. White silk satin trimmed with beading and silver gauze. Worn by Bertha Brown to marry Zadik Heiber in London. Given by Enid Wistrich.
T.459:1, 2-1996

1923
Dress and train. Oyster silk satin decorated with beaded satin petals. Worn by Christina, the bride of Mr Hyde. Given by Mrs K.C. Hyde.
T.212 to B-1987

1924
Dress. White silk satin with bead embroidery. Designed by Claire of Connaught Place, London. Worn by Henrietta Frances Ruth Akers to marry Lewis Gordon Campbell in London in January. Given by Mrs Campbell.
T.38 to B-1951

1924
Dress. Pleated chiffon and ivory silk satin embroidered with pearls and crystals. Bandeau headdress of pearl beads. Worn by the bride of Mr Gerelli in London. Given by the Misses J. & L. Watt.
T.252, 253-1968

1926
Dress. Ivory georgette embroidered with silver and crystals. Net veil with orange-blossom wreath. Designed by Mrs Handley-Seymour, London. Worn by the bride of Mr Koppenhagen in Hampstead, London. Given by Mrs A Kay.
T.25&B, C-1973

1927
Dress. Gold silk velvet

T.71A, B-1982

embroidered with pearl beads. Worn by Maud Katharine Alicia Cecil for her marriage to Richard Greville Acton Steel at St Margaret's, Westminster, London, on 17 November. Given by Oriel and Alicia Robinson.
T.126-2009

1928
Dress. Ivory silk satin beaded with glass pearls. Designed and made by Lady Frazer, Tientsin, China. Worn by the donor's daughter in China in January. Given by Mrs Minnie Bremner.
T.126 to C-1936

1928
Blue wool coat reversing to printed silk. Matching printed silk dress. Blue felt cloche hat with ostrich feathers. Designed by Liberty & Co. London. Worn by Marian Hazel Lasenby to marry William Moorcroft at

St George's, Hanover Square,
London.
T.71 to B-1982

1928
Dress. White tulle embroidered
with diamanté.
Made by Cope of Harrogate.
Worn by Cecelie Perlin to marry
Harold Rowe in Liverpool,
Lancashire.
Given by Miss Ann Rowe in memory
of her mother, Cecelie Perlin.
T.374&A-1990

1929–30
Three-piece suit. Pink marocain
with satin appliqués.
Designed by Jeanne Lanvin, Paris.
Worn by Marie Harvey for her
second marriage to Mr Reed.
Given by Mrs Reed on behalf of
Mrs Harvey.
T.202 to C-1931

1930s

1931
Top-hat. Black silk.
Made by Lincoln Bennet & Co.,
Sackville Street, London.
Worn by Dr Henry Emmanuel
Compton to marry Clarice Kahne
at the Masonic Rooms,
Huddersfield, Yorkshire, on
15 April.
Given by Barbara S. Rantzen.
T.41:1 to 4-2004

1932
Dress. Champagne silk satin and
tulle embroidered with pearls and
metal thread.
Designed by Norman Hartnell,
London, and purchased in New
York, USA in 1931.
Worn by Mrs Dorothy Miller for her
marriage.
Given by Margaret D. Wishart.
T.623:1, 2-1999

1932
Dress. White crêpe trimmed with
piqué daisies. Sequin cap and net
veil. Camisole of silk crêpe
trimmed with lace.
Dress designed by Victor Stiebel,
London.
Headdress designed by Jeanne
Lanvin, Paris.
Camisole made by Hermine Ltd,
London.
Worn by Joan Pearson to marry
Anthony Acton in London.
Given by Mrs Anthony Acton.
T.71, 72-1966; T.227-1969

1933
Dress. Ivory silk satin and tulle,
embroidered with pearls.
Designed by Norman Hartnell,

T.215 I, J-1953

London.
Worn by Margaret Whigham to
marry Charles Sweeny at the
Brompton Oratory, London, on
21 February.
Given and worn by Margaret,
Duchess of Argyll.
T.836-1974

1934
Dress. Cream silk velvet.
Embroidered net veil.
Worn by Freda Sylvia Benoly to
marry Vivian A.S. Vokes at
St Matthew's Parish Church,
Bethnal Green, London, on
29 September.
Given by Mrs L.D. Benoly.
T.11 to C-1940

1934
Dress. Bias-cut cream silk satin
with double train.
Designed by Charles James,
London.
Worn by Barbara 'Baba' Jessica
Hardy Beaton to marry Alec
Hambro at St Mark's Church,
North Audley Street, London, on
6 November.
Given by Mrs Alec Hambro.
T.271-1974

1935
Dress and train. Cream jersey
velvet. Net veil with wax orange-
blossom wreath. Silk stockings.
Cream velvet shoes. Cream satin
underwear with coffee lace
insertions.
Worn by Mary Magdalene
Dresbach to marry William
Llewellyn Craig at the Church of
St Ignatius, Intramures, Manila,
Philippines, on 12 February.
Given by Patricia Craig.
T.39:1 to 18-1999

1935
Dress. Pink machine-embroidered
net. Pink satin slip. Net veil.
Beaded headdress and matching

earrings. White satin and silver kid
shoes.
Shoes retailed by Jack Jacobus
Ltd.
Worn and given by Hilary Lyme
Murdoch.
T.215 to J-1953

1936
Dress. White silk satin
embroidered with beads. Matching
clutch bag.
Possibly designed by Worth.
Worn by the donor's mother.
Given by Mrs Belinda Harding.
T.277&A-1985

1937
Dress. Bias-cut cream silk satin.
Designed by Gaby Bernier, Canada.
Given by Mrs N. Longden.
T.270-1984

1938
Headdress. Wax orange-blossom.
Retailed by Liberty & Co., London.
Worn by Maisie Violet Swain to
marry Cecil Denis Bradley Moon in
Wembley, Middlesex, on 4 June.
Given by Hilary Moon.
T.212:1 to 4-1996

1938
Dress. Red silk gauze over
matching artificial silk slip.
Dark blue silk belt.

T.212:1-1996

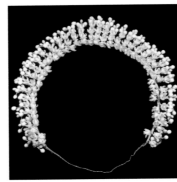

Worn by Helen Monica Maurice to
marry Dr Arthur Newton Jackson
at the Chapel of Our Lady,
Rotheram, Yorkshire, in June.
Given by the family of Monica
Maurice.
T.716:1 to 3-1995

1940s

1940
Hat. Purple velvet trimmed with
artificial violets.
Made in Paris and retailed by
Harrods, London.
Worn by the donor for her
marriage in London in March.
Worn and given by Mrs Josephine
Reed.
T.20-1973

1941
Dress. Cream satin furnishing
fabric woven with buttercups.
Headdress of yellow artificial
flowers with net veil.
Designed by Ella Dolling, Portland
Street, London.
Worn by Elizabeth King to marry
Ralph Rowland Absalom at
St John's Church, Hyde Park
Square, London, on 6 September.
Given by Mrs Gay Oliver Barrett.
T.25:1 to 5-2006

1942
Suit. Slate-blue wool crêpe dress
and jacket trimmed with grey
astrakhan.
Retailed by Marshall & Snelgrove,
Birmingham.
Worn by Margaret Harper to marry
Oliver Frank Spinney at St Giles's
Church, Rowley Regis, West
Midlands.
Given anonymously.
T.50:1, 2-2008

1944
Dress. Heavy white 'parachute'
silk. Beaded pillbox hat.
Designed by Helen Drew.
Worn by Madame Albrecht for her
wedding at St Matthew's Church,
Surbiton, Surrey, on 29 April.
Given by Mme Sheila Albrecht.
T.134&A-1975

1946
Bodice. Ivory satin quilted with
pearls. Matching pillbox hat.
Bodice designed by Pierre
Balmain, Paris.
Hat by Paulette, Paris.
Worn by Stella Carcano y Morra to
marry William Humble David
Ward, 4th Earl of Dudley,
on 10 January.
Given by Stella, Lady Ednam.
T.46&A-1974

1947

Dress. Draped white synthetic jersey. Elbow-length gloves in kid leather.
Worn by Joyce R. Afriat to marry Henry Natanson at the Spanish & Portuguese Synagogue, Landrake Road, Maida Vale, London, on 7 November.
Given by Mr Raymond Natanson.
T.560:1 to 3-1997

1947

Dress. White artificial figured silk. Wax orange-blossom wreath.
Designed by Marie of Luton.
Worn by Marie Vidoykovitch to marry Howard Everett at Letchworth Free Church, Hertfordshire, on 21 June.
T.232:1, 2-1998

1947

Hat. Blue ostrich feathers and pink velvet roses.
Made by Paul Walser Ltd (Reslaw).
Worn by the donor's mother to marry Alec Lower at the Coventry Registry Office, Warwickshire, on 12 July.
Given by Mrs E.M. Northover.
T.42-1996

1948

Dress and jacket. Blue and white printed rayon. Navy straw hat. Navy patent leather handbag. Navy leather sandals.
Dress and jacket designed by Elspeth Champcommunal for Worth London.
Worn by the donor's mother.
Given by Diana C. Briscoe.
T.536 to 540-1993

1948

Dress. Pale grey-blue silk figured with carnations.
Designed by Edward Molyneux,

T.42-1996

London.
Worn by Esme Ethel Alice Walker (née d'Beaumont) for her second marriage to Sir Wykeham Stanley Cornwallis, 2nd Baron Cornwallis on 26 February.
Given by the 3rd Lord and Lady Cornwallis.
T.295-1984

1948

Dress. White watered silk. White watered silk sandals. Silk net veil.
Designed by Edward Molyneux, London.
Sandals made by Rayne, London.
Worn by Patricia Aileen Cunningham to marry Charles Creed at the Assumption Convent, Kensington Square, London, on 1 September.
T.250 to E-1979

1949

Skirt suit. Red wool trimmed with black braid.
Retailed by Bon Marché, Liverpool.
Worn by Rachel Ginsburg to marry Walter Foster at the Brondesbury Synagogue, London, on 4 January.
Given by Mrs W. Foster.
T.14&A-1960

1950s

1951

Dress. Silk satin embroidered with bands of pearls, crystals and sequins.
Designed by Norman Hartnell, London.
Worn by Hermione Wills to marry Mervyn Evans at St Mark's, North Audley Street, London, on 23 July.
Given by Mrs H.S. Ball.
T.217&A-1972

1954

Dress. Cotton organza with Swiss embroidery.
Designed by Horrockses, Preston and London.
Worn by Pamela M. Taylor to marry Keith Ashworth at St Cuthbert's Church, Southport, Lancashire.
Given by Mrs P.M. Ashworth.
T.166:1 to 7-1997

1954

Dress and jacket. Brown wool worsted figured with gold lurex.
Designed by Jacques Fath, Paris.
Worn by Lady Alexandra Howard-Johnston for her second marriage to Hugh Trevor-Roper on 4 October.
Given by Lady Alexandra Trevor-Roper.
T.178&A-1974

1955

'Martian's Claw' headdress. Sculptural form covered with net and metal spangles.

T.178&A-1974

Designed by Lachasse, London.
Worn and given by Mrs June Gordan-Gottschalk.
T.398-1988

1956

Handbag. Metal and faux pearl box-shaped minaudière.
Made by Fiorella.
Carried by Carol Mitzman to marry Jeffrey Howard at the Dollis Hill Synagogue, London, on 26 December.
Given by Carol Howard.
T.234:1 to 3-1998

1957

Ballerina-length dress. Ivory satin overlaid with pearl-embroidered lace. Satin clutch bag.
Designed by Norman Hartnell, London.
Worn by Mrs Laurel Heath for her second marriage to Mr Gerald Albertini at St James's Roman Catholic Church, Spanish Place, London, on 25 June.
Given by Laurel Robinson.
T.530-1996; T.152:1 to 3-2000

1957

Dress. Heavy textured cream silk. Nylon lace corset. Net veil. Nylon petticoat trimmed with lace.
Dress designed by Jacques Fath, Paris, for Vogue Couturier Patterns and made up by a private dressmaker.
Corset manufactured by Berlei.
Worn by Vivian Albany Williams to marry Mr Ward in Wood Green, Middlesex, on 3 August.
Given by Mrs Ward.
T.16:1 to 3-1991; T.102-2009

1959

Wedding veil. Machine embroidered net.
Designed by Alison Erridge for

T.398-1988

Worth London.
CIRC.298-1962

1960s

1960

Dress and jacket. Machine-embroidered champagne satin. Veil of champagne net. Gold leather shoes.
Dress designed by Eileen Andrews, London.
Veil designed by John Boyd, London.
Shoes made by the London Shoe Company.
Worn by Frances Barrett to marry Mr M.H.N. Plaisted on 20 August.
Given by Mrs Frances Plaisted.
T.464:1 to 5-1997

1961

Dress. Cream satin embroidered with beads and chenille.
Designed by Owen Hyde Clark for

T.46A-1974

Worth London.
Worn by the donor for her wedding at St John's Wood Church, Westminster, London, on 18 November.
Given anonymously.
T.868-1974

1962
Short dress. White ribbed satin. Headdress of nylon net trimmed with pearls, artificial flowers and satin ribbon.
Designed and worn by Wendy Ramshaw to marry David Watkins at Christ Church, Sunderland, Tyne & Wear, 12 August.
Given by Wendy Ramshaw.
T.49:1, 2-2010

1963
Dress. Ivory silk shantung. Matching silk shantung cap with net veil.
Designed by Jacques Heim, Paris, and made up in London.
Worn by Edith April Oehlrichs for her marriage in London in March.
Worn and given by April Olrich.
T.404:1, 2-2001

1963
Dress. Cream watered silk. Designed by Victor Stiebel for his final collection, London.
Given by Victor Stiebel.
T.169-1973

1964
Dress. White silk satin overlaid with organza.
Designed by Belinda Bellville and David Sassoon for Bellville et Cie.
Worn by Anne Stephen to marry Allan Berkeley Valentine Hughes, in London on 24 April.
Given by Allan Hughes.
T.403:1, 2-2001

1966
Minidress and coat. White cotton gabardine and silvered PVC.
Designed by John Bates at Jean
T.30:1, 2-2010

Varon.
Worn by Marit Allen to marry Sandy Lieberson at St Mary's Church, The Boltons, Chelsea, London, on 10 June.
T.26:1, 2-2009

1967
Frock coat and trousers. Grey wool. Designed by Mr Fish, London.
Worn by Charles Evelyn Penn Lucas to marry Antoinette von Westenholz at the Church of the Immaculate Conception, Farm St., London, on 9 November.
T.30:1, 2-2010

1968
Coat-dress. Cream silk cloqué trimmed with Arctic fox fur.
Designed by Belinda Bellville and David Sassoon for Bellville et Cie.
Worn for a wedding on 28 December.
T.82-1988

1969
'Lamborghini' trouser suit. Cream satin jacket with black, cream and gold printed satin trousers.
Trouser suit designed by Ossie Clark.
Fabric designed by Celia Birtwell.
Worn and given by Hilary Milne.
T.472:1, 2-1997

1969
Dress. White wool trimmed with braid. Headdress of braided fabric strips. Shoes covered in ivory crêpe with ribbon and pearl rosettes.
Dress designed by Jean Muir, London.
Headdress designed by Graham Smith, London.
Shoes made by Dal Co., Italy.
Worn by Pamela Talmey Colin to marry William David Ormsby-Gore, 5th Baron Harlech, at the Grosvenor Chapel, Mayfair, London, on 11 December.
Given by Pamela, Lady Harlech.
T.268 to C-1986

1970s

1970
Dress. Layers of cream organza and antique lace. Matching cap. Posy of artificial flowers.
Designed by Gina Fratini, London.
Given by Gina Fratini.
T.194 to B-1974

1970
'Faye Dunaway' dress. Cream machine lace, satin and devoré velvet.

Designed by Thea Porter, London.
Worn by Susanne Trill to marry James David Elliot in Lincolnshire on 21 March.
Given by Susanne Elliot.
T.46:1 to 3-2005

1970
Dress. White silk chiffon with pale pink and orange print.
Designed by Zandra Rhodes, London.
Worn by Laura Beare to marry David Gebber at Hampstead Synagogue, London, on 5 July.
Given by Laura Beare.
T.105:1, 2-2009

1970
Dress. White synthetic satin. Hooded coat of machine-made lace.
Retailed by Berketex, UK.
Worn by Susan Fryer to marry Stephen Smith at Wembley Park Congregational Church, Middlesex, on 1 September.
Given by Mrs Susan Evans.
T.48:1, 2-2010

1970
'Rajputana' coat. Hand-painted white wool crêpe.
Painted by Andrew Whittle.
Designed by Richard Cawley for Bellville Sassoon, London, 1970. The coat came from the Autumn/Winter 1970–71 couture collection.
Worn by Sara Donaldson-Hudson to marry Nicholas Haydon at the Caxton Hall registry office, Westminster, London, on 23 April 1971.
Given by Mr David Sassoon.
T.26-2006

1972
Evening dress. Blue crêpe with enamel bee buttons.
Designed by Bill Gibb, London.
Worn by the donor for her November wedding.
Given by Mrs Angela Dixon.
T.172-1986

1973
Evening dress. Purple moss crêpe. Straw hat trimmed with flowers.
Dress designed by Ossie Clark, London.
Hat designed by Diane Logan, London.
Worn and given by Frances Hinchcliffe.
T.430-1988; T.14-1982

T.32:2-2006

1975
Dress. White linen. Cream satin shoes. Nylon net hat trimmed with fabric flowers and chiffon.
Dress designed by Geoffrey Beene, New York.
Shoes designed by Herbert Levine, New York.
Hat designed by Frank Clive, New York.
Worn by Catharina Oeschger to marry Peter Tinniswood at St Nicholas' Church, Thames Ditton, Surrey, on 9 August.
Given by Catharina Tinniswood.
T.32:1 to 4-2006

1975–80
Dress. Cream quilted silk with hand-painted flowers. Matching headband.
Designed by Cindy Beadman.
Given by the designer.
T.876:1 to 3-2000

1975–80
Dress. White silk crinoline decorated with embroidered and cutwork snowflakes. White quilted silk crown.
Designed by Cindy Beadman.
Given by the designer.
T.875:1 to 3-2000

1976
Dress. White organza and artificial flowers. Net crinoline. Headdress of artificial flowers with attached tulle veil.

T.181 to G-1980

Designed by Mrs Spiegel for
Neymar, London.
Embroidered by Lock & Co, London.
Worn by Angela Stamp to marry
Howard Fineman on 15 August.
Given by Angela Fineman.
T.148:1 to 3-2004

1976
Dress. Pale yellow printed and
pleated silk chiffon with satin sash,
decorated with sequins.
Designed by Zandra Rhodes,
London.
Worn by Elizabeth Florence Weiner
to marry David Emanuel.
Given by Elizabeth Emanuel.
T.9:1 to 5-2006

1977
Dress. White cotton trimmed with
heavy cotton lace.
Made by Laura Ashley Ltd, Wales.
Worn by Alina Stankowski to marry
Dave Gribbin in Durham.
Given by Mrs A. Gribbin.
T.287-1982

1979
Dress. Ivory and pink silk taffeta
trimmed with bows and artificial
flowers. Sequinned tulle veil.
Wreath of artificial flowers.
Designed by David and Elizabeth
Emanuel for Liberty's 'Silk Cut'
show, December 1979.
Given by David and Elizabeth
Emanuel.
T.181 to G-1980

1980s

1987
Dress. White lace over satin.
Headdress of cream satin roses
with tulle veil.
Dress designed by Victor
Edelstein, London.
Veil and headdress designed by
Frederick Fox, London.
Worn by Miss Marilyn Watts to
marry Mr Bloomfield.
Given by Miss Marilyn Watts.
T.100 to B-1988

1987
Ensemble. White rayon dress and
coat trimmed with silk and
organza roses. Organza blouse.
Headdress. Cream silk shoes with
large bows.
Outfit designed by John Galliano,
London.
Shoes designed by Patrick Cox,
London.
Worn by Francesca Oddi for her
marriage at Ampthill,
Bedfordshire.
Worn and given by Francesca Oddi.
T.41 to C-1988

T.371:1 to 3-2009

1989
Dress and coat. Pleated white silk.
Net veil painted with silicone
rubber. Pleated silk shoes.
Designed by Ian & Marcel, London.
Shoes made by Hanna Goldman.
T.178:1 to 5-1993

1990s

1990
'Spacebaby' dress and shawl.
Transparent PVC.
Designed by John McKitterick for
Red or Dead's first catwalk show,
London.
Given by the designer.
T.159 to B-1990

1992
Dress. Heavy white crêpe with cut-
away sides and back, applied
beading.
Designed by Bruce Oldfield,
London.
Worn by Lisa Butcher to marry
Marco Pierre White at the
Brompton Oratory, South
Kensington, London, on 15 August.
Given by Ms Julia Bridges.
T.198-1997

1992
'Farewell, Sweet Liberty' dress.
Ivory raw silk trimmed with studs,
pearls, rivets and chains.
Designed by Joe Casely-Hayford
for Liberty.
Given by Liberty & Co. Ltd.
T.323-1993

1992
'Qui a le droit?' wedding dress.
White and black satin, tulle and
organza embroidered with

coloured chenille, metallic thread
and glass gems. Black satin shoes.
Black tulle veil. Black silk gloves.
Rings and hair ornaments of glass
gems set in gilt metal.
Designed by Christian Lacroix,
Paris for his Autumn/Winter
1992–3 Haute Couture collection.
Shoes made by Sidonie Larizzi,
Paris.
Given by the designer.
T.241:1 to 16-1993

1993
Caftan. Cream silk smocked and
embroidered with beads and
ribbons.
Designed by Julian Mary Akers-
Douglas.
Given by the designer.
T.528-1993

1996
Wedding ensemble. Red and black
quilted silk evening skirt. White
piqué corset. Red silk shoes
trimmed with faux zebra fur.
Skirt designed by Pearce Fionda,
London, 1995.
Corset designed by Vivienne
Westwood, London, 1996.
Shoes designed by Jimmy Choo,
London, 1996.
Worn and given by Jane Levi.
T.13 to 15-2002

1996
'Rosalind' wedding shoes. Cream
satin trimmed with crêpe roses
and pearls.
Designed by Diane Hassall.
Given by the designer.
T.186:1, 2-1996

1996
Wedding shoes. Silver metallic
organza.
Designed by Claire Norwood.
Given by the designer.
T.154:1, 2-1996

1996
Dress. Shell pink satin.
Designed by Catherine Rayner,
London.
Given by the designer.
T.15-1997

1996
Dress. Ivory silk zibeline and
organza.
Designed by Phillipa Lepley,
London.
Given by the designer.
T.529-1996

1996
Ecological wedding dress. Hand-
embroidered natural undyed hemp
and silk blend fabric. Shawl to

match. Pillbox hat of palm fibre
trimmed with silk roses.
Alternative headdress of natural
silk chiffon and ribbons. Brown
leather sandals.
Designed by Veronica Schwandt for
Hess Naturtextilien, Germany.
Sandals made by Schuh Werk,
Germany.
Given by Hess Naturtextilien.
T.85:1 to 9-2000

1998
Dress. Ivory beaded lace. Veil of
tulle with beaded lace headband.
White silk shoes.
Dress and veil designed by
Deborah Milner, London.
Shoes designed by Jacques
Azagury, London.
Worn by Estelle Skornik as 'Nicole'
in the Renault television
advertisement first screened
29 May 1998.
Given by Renault UK Ltd.
T.40:1 to 4-2000

21st century

2006
Two-piece suit. Dark grey wool
with blue and white fleck. Blue and
white cotton shirt.
Suit designed by Kilgour, Savile
Row, London.
Shirt designed by Jasper Conran.
Worn by Christopher Breward for
his civil partnership ceremony
with James Brook in London
on 18 August.
Given by Christopher Breward and
James Brook.
T.371:1 to 3-2009

2006
Two-piece suit. Dark grey wool-
blend with blue pinstripe. White
cotton shirt with blue and red
stripe.
Designed by Timothy Everest for
Marks & Spencer.
Shirt made by T.M. Lewin.
Worn by James Brook for his civil
partnership ceremony with
Christopher Breward in London on
18 August.
Given by Christopher Breward and
James Brook.
T.372:1 to 3-2009

2007
Dress. White silk tissue, satin-
faced organza and tulle.
Designed by Vera Wang for her
Spring 2007 Bridal Collection.
Worn by Katie Bella Turner to
marry Andrew Robert Hayward at
the Old Field Club, Setauket,
New York, USA, on 26 August.
LOAN.AMERICANFRIENDS:569-2009

GLOSSARY

BASQUE An extension of the bodice below the waist

BLOCK PRINT A print in which the pattern is transferred onto the fabric with wooden blocks (on which the pattern has been cut in relief)

BLOND LACE A generic term for bobbin lace, made originally from undyed cream silk, but also from black and white silk

BOBBIN LACE A generic term for all lace made by plaiting or twisting together a number of threads wound on small bobbins and secured at the upper ends to a hard pillow

BROCADING A type of weave in which a motif or design is created by adding extra weft threads. They do not run across the width of the textile but are added only where they are required for the pattern

BUCKRAM An open-textured, stiffened linen or cotton cloth used for linings

CHEMISETTE A white cotton bodice, with open side seams, worn under low-cut day dresses for modesty and cleanliness. Some have collars; those without were worn with the upper edge partially visible

CLOQUÉ A cloth with a blistered effect, produced by embossing or stamping the fabric, or by using yarns that shrink at different rates

CRINOLINE Fabric woven from horsehair and cotton or linen, used to stiffen, or add volume to petticoats. By 1856 the term was also used for an under-garment hanging from the waist made from graduated, shaped hoops designed to support the skirt according to the fashionable silhouette. From 1857 watch-spring was used to make the hoops. The term 'crinoline cage' was also used for this supporting garment

DAMASK A fabric whose pattern is created by the juxtaposition of the two faces of a weave, usually satin weave

FAILLE A slightly ribbed, woven fabric of silk, cotton or rayon

FLY FRINGE An eighteenth-century trimming made from floss (untwisted) silk cut into short lengths and knotted together to form a core onto which further short lengths are knotted to create fluffy tufts of silk

FROCK COAT (FROCK) At the end of the eighteenth century, a man's frock coat was one with a turned-down collar and tails. From about 1816 the term was used for a man's close-fitting, knee-length coat

GLACÉ A fabric with a glossy, lustrous surface

GROSGRAIN A type of weave in which silk warp threads are woven over thicker weft threads of silk or cotton to achieve a ribbed effect

HOOP PETTICOAT An eighteenth-century under-petticoat of linen shaped with cane or whalebone hoops

KERCHIEF An abbreviation of handkerchief or neckerchief. The term was used in the eighteenth century to describe a square or triangular piece of silk, cotton, linen or lace worn around the shoulders and chest

LAMÉ A general term for textiles containing a weft of metallic thread

LAPPETS A pair of long streamers, often of lace, attached to a cap. They were worn in various ways, pinned up and hanging down, depending on fashion

MOIRÉ A watered effect made on a ribbed fabric by folding and applying high pressure, which causes some ribs to flatten, reflecting the light unevenly

MUSLIN A very fine, light-weight sheer cotton

NEEDLE LACE Lace made with a needle and thread

OMBRÉ BLOCK Block used to print colours, which are laid out in stripes and allowed to merge into each other at the edges, creating gradations, rather than solid colour effects

OPEN GOWN An eighteenth-century term for a gown whose skirt is open at the front to reveal the petticoat worn underneath

ORANGE-BLOSSOM The small, white, fragrant flowers of the orange tree. Artificial orange-blossom was variously made from wax, cloth and paper

ORGANDIE A thin, plain-weave cotton fabric with a stiff finish

ORGANZA A sheer silk, stiff to handle, woven from silk with its natural gum intact

PASSEMENTERIE A generic French term for a wide range of trimmings used to decorate and finish upholstery or dress. It includes braid, cord, tassels and fringing

PELISSE A woman's front-fastening, full-length outer garment designed to be worn like a coat

PELISSE-ROBE A woman's day dress in the form of a pelisse. The centre front closes with fastenings until just above the hem, where the seam is closed

PEPLUM A gathered and pleated piece of fabric attached to the waist of a woman's dress or jacket to create a decorative or drapery effect

PETTICOAT This term is used in the eighteenth century for a skirt which formed part of an outer garment such as a gown

PIQUÉ A white cotton fabric with a self-coloured slightly raised surface pattern

PLAIN WEAVE The simplest form of weaving, in which the weft crosses regularly over and under each warp. Also called 'tabby'

POINT DE GAZE Mid-nineteenth-century name for a new form of Brussels needle lace with a gauzy net ground and naturalistic floral patterns

POINT LACE Although used originally to describe needle lace, by the eighteenth century the term was used more generally for certain types of needle lace and Brussels bobbin lace. In the nineteenth century it was used even more broadly, sometimes to indicate hand- rather than machine-made lace

POPLIN A plain-weave ribbed fabric, made from various fibres

SACK-BACK A style of eighteenth-century woman's gown with the fabric at the back arranged in box pleats at the shoulders and falling loose to the floor with a slight train

SATIN A weave structure in which the warp covers the weft on the surface of the cloth, creating a fabric with a smooth, glossy surface

STAND COLLAR An upright collar of a coat, waistcoat or dress, constructed without a turn-down

THREAD LACE Any form of bobbin lace made with a linen thread. The term was used in the eighteenth century to denote a cheap, simple form of lace made from less finely spun linen thread

TISSUE A complex weave with additional warps and wefts used for decorative effect

TOBY TUB A specially constructed 'sieve' used in block-printing. A wooden block is carved into compartments which correspond in shape, size and position to the different elements of the pattern on the wood block. The separate compartments are then filled with different colours according to the design of the print

TULLE A very fine net fabric made from silk yarn

TWILL A weave in which the warp threads float over two or more weft threads, or vice versa, creating a diagonal effect

WARP Strong structural threads running the length of the fabric from end to end

WATERED See 'moiré'

WEFT The threads which run from side to side of a fabric, under and over the warp threads

WHITEWORK A generic term used for white linen or cotton decorated with embroidery, lace or net executed in white thread

ZIBELINE A heavy, lustrous twill-weave silk

NOTES

EPIGRAPH

1. Cited in Gillian Lenfestey, 'An Alderney Wedding 1779', *Costume* (2003), vol. 37, pp.66–70

INTRODUCTION

1. V&A: T.175&A–1900. See Natalie Rothstein (ed.), *Four Hundred Years of Fashion* (London, 1984), pp.53–4. The attribution of the suit to Sir Thomas Isham's wedding has been questioned as no reference to it has been found in inventories of his clothes.

2. V&A: T.939&A–1902. The silk dates to 1755–60 and the construction of the dress to the late 1770s or 1780s. The dress is small and may have been made from silk unpicked from an earlier dress and petticoat, or a piece of unused silk.

3. The V&A has one wedding outfit worn by a member of the royal family. This is the suit worn by James, Duke of York (later King James II of England and VII of Scotland) (1633–1701) for the confirmation of his marriage contract with Mary of Modena (1658–1718) which took place on her arrival in England on 21 November 1673 at Dover. The Duke had married his wife by proxy in Italy in September 1673. V&A: T.711:1, 2–1995

4. Phillis Cunnington and Catherine Lucas, *Costume for Births, Marriages and Deaths* (London, 1972), pp.41–3, 55

5. Ibid., pp.146–7, 246–8, 270–2, 277

6. Office for National Statistics (ONS), Provisional report of marriages registered in England and Wales, and the United Kingdom as a whole, in 2008, http://www.statistics.gov.uk (accessed 3 August 2010)

7. For discussions about the defining qualities of English and British fashion, see Alison Settle, *English Fashion* (London, 1948); Christopher Breward, Becky Conekin and Caroline Cox, *The Englishness of English Dress* (Oxford and New York, 2002); and Alison Goodrum, *The National Fabric: Fashion, Britishness, Globalization (Dress, Body, Culture)* (Oxford and New York, 2005).

8. Harriet Simons Williams, 'Eliza Lucas and Her Family: Before the Letterbook', *South Carolina Historical Magazine* (July 1998), vol. 99, no. 3, pp.265–6

9. 'Farlington', *Hampshire Telegraph and Sussex Chronicle* (19 August 1854)

10. Justine Picardie, *The Fabric of Our Lives* (London, 2005), pp.2–15

11. ONS, 'Provisional report of marriages'

CHAPTER ONE

1. Amanda Vickery, *The Gentleman's Daughter* (New Haven and London, 1998), pp.41–5

2. Ibid., p.39

3. Elizabeth Einberg, *Manners and Morals: Hogarth and British Painting 1700–60* (Tate Gallery, exhib. cat., 1987), pp.160–1

4. Ann Monsarrat, *And the Bride Wore … The Story of the White Wedding* (London, 1973), p.57. 'Private marryings' that avoided the calling of banns in church and a public ceremony were particularly popular in London. See Peter Earle, *A City Full of People: Men and Women of London 1650–1750* (London, 1994), p.157

5. Irregular marriages did take place but they fall outside the scope of this book. For the marriage acts and marriage law in the eighteenth century, see Rebecca Probert, *Marriage Law and Practice in the Long Eighteenth Century: A Reassessment* (Cambridge, 2009).

6. Margaret Blundell (ed.), *Blundell's Diary and Letter Book 1702–28* (Liverpool, 1952), p.11. Nicholas Blundell of Crosby Hall in Lancashire wore a blue coat, waistcoat and breeches with silver buttons when he married in 1703. In a 1762 novel by Tobias Smollett, when Sir Lancelot Greaves marries Miss Darnel he wears a 'white coat and blue sattin vest, both embroidered with silver' (*The Life and Adventures of Sir Lancelot Greaves* (Oxford, 1926), p.286).

7. Einberg (1987), pp.73–4. The church in this painting is not where Stephen Beckingham and Mary Cox married, but the recently completed interior of St Martin-in-the-Fields which was close to the St Martin's Lane Academy of which Hogarth was a leading member.

8. Monsarrat (1973), pp.92–5

9. Nigel Surry (ed.), *'Your affectionate and loving sister': The correspondence of Barbara Kerrich and Elizabeth Postlethwaite 1733 to 1751* (Dereham, 2000), pp.80–1

10. William Ffolkes joined Gray's Inn in 1717 and the Middle Temple in 1720, later becoming Registrar of the Alienation Office. Mary was his second wife. He had four daughters from his previous marriage and he and Mary had a son.

11. Wrest Park Papers, Bedfordshire County Record Office, L/31/137–8, cited in Anne Buck, *Dress in Eighteenth-Century England* (London, 1979), p.158. There were twenty shillings in a pound and twelve pence in a shilling.

12. Earle (1994), p.123

13. Wrest Park Papers, L/31/137–8, cited in Buck (1979), p.158

14. Miles Lambert, '"Sent From Town": Commissioning Clothing in Britain during the Long Eighteenth Century', *Costume* (2009), vol. 43, pp.80–1; See also Buck (1979), pp.73–4 which describes a commission in 1760 when relatives of the bride's future husband purchased a white silk damask sprigged with a few coloured flowers for her wedding dress.

15. James Greig (ed.), *The Diaries of a Duchess: Extracts from the Diaries of the First Duchess of Northumberland (1716–1776)* (London, 1926), pp.31–2

16. Wrest Park Papers, L/30/11/240/6, cited in Buck (1979), p.161. When Mary, youngest daughter of Marchioness Grey, went shopping in London to choose silk for her wedding clothes in 1780, she was looking for white and silver, with white and gold as an alternative and white satin as a fallback. Disappointed in her first choice, she settled for white and gold.

17. Lady Llanover (ed.), *The Autobiography and Correspondence of Mary Granville, Mrs Delany* (London, 1861), series 1, vol.1, pp.427–8

18. Llanover (1862), series 2, vol.2, p.341

19. Hannah Greig, 'Dressing for Court: Sartorial Politics and Fashion News in the Age of Mary Delany' in Mark Laird and Alicia Weisberg-Roberts (eds), *Mrs Delany and Her Circle* (New Haven and London, 2009), pp.88–9

20. V&A: T.260&A–1969

21. Eighteenth-century gardening books written for women often describe the cultural meanings of plants and flowers as well as their uses. See, for example, Charles Evelyn, *The Lady's Recreation; or, the third and last part of the Art of Gardening Improv'd* (London, 1717), pp.116–7: 'And Cato mentions a Myrtle, called by the name Conjugal Myrtle'.

22. V&A: T.374, 376–1972

23. V&A: T.939&A–1902. See Shelley Tobin, Sarah Pepper and Margaret Willes, *Marriage à la Mode: Three Centuries of Wedding Dress* (London, 2003), pp.16–18, 20–21; Jane Tozer and Sarah Levitt, *Fabric of Society: A Century of People and their Clothes 1770–1870* (Carno, 1983), p.49; and Linda Baumgarten, *What Clothes Reveal: The Language of Clothing in Colonial and Federal America* (New Haven and London, 2002), p.8

24. Tozer and Levitt (1983), pp.47–8

25. Grace Evans, '*Mariage à la Mode*: An Eighteenth-Century Wedding Dress, Hat and Shoes Set from the Olive Matthews Collection, Chertsey Museum', *Costume* (2008), vol. 42, pp.50–65

26. Aileen Ribeiro, *Dress in Eighteenth-Century Europe 1715–89* (London, 1984), p.157

27. Monsarrat (1973), p.96. The bride wore a style of dress known as a nightgown which, though informal, could be made from rich fabrics. It was often worn for daytime weddings.

CHAPTER TWO

1. W.S. Lewis and A. Dayle Wallace (eds), *Horace Walpole's Correspondence with Mary and Agnes Berry, and Barbara Cecilia Seton* (London, 1944), p.255

2. Deirdre Le Faye, *Jane Austen's 'Outlandish Cousin': The Life and Letters of Eliza de Feuillide* (London, 2002), p.137, letter dated 3 May 1797. The Princess Royal, the eldest daughter of George III, married the Prince of Württemberg on 18 May 1797.

3. *The Times* (17 April 1797)

4. 'Selections', *Observer* (14 May 1797)

5. Venetia Murray, *High Society: A Social History of the Regency Period, 1788–1830* (London, 1998), pp.78–9

6. 'The Mirror of Fashion', *Morning Chronicle* (22 December 1806)

7. 'Incidents occurring In or Near London, Interesting Marriages etc.', *La Belle Assemblée and Bell's Court and Fashionable Magazine* (March 1812). A guinea was worth £1 1s.

8. 'Household Establishments', Chatsworth Estate, 1811, cited in Murray (1998), p.68

9. In 1817 those who could claim the privilege of marrying by special licence included bishops and their children, peers and peeresses and their children, privy councillors and their children, members and ex-members of parliament and their children, great officers of state, baronets and their children, knights, knight commanders of the Order of the Bath, and those having a patent or warrant from the crown, judges and their children, counsel of the crown, deans, generals and admirals, court physicians and surgeons, officers of the royal household, officers of the vice-regal household and doctors of divinity. John Cordy Jeaffreson, *Brides and Bridals* (London,1872), vol.1, pp.134–5

10. In April 1816 Mrs Griffin, a dressmaker in Ryder Street near St James's Palace, printed an announcement stating that she had 'just returned from Paris with a variety of elegant & new designs, and having brought a Milliner of great taste and ability from one of the principal Marchandes de mode in Paris has reason to hope she will be able to give the greatest satisfaction.' British Museum, Banks Collection: D2:3037

11. 'Grand Magazin de Modes', Advertisements and Notices, *Morning Chronicle* (15 March 1819). The advertisement promises a great assortment of embroideries of every description, superb marriage gowns, an assortment of French artificial flowers, ball gowns, trimmings and all novelties received every week.

12. Fiona Ffoulkes, ' "Quality always distinguishes itself": Louis Hippolyte LeRoy and the Luxury Clothing Industry in Early Nineteenth-Century Paris' in Maxine Berg and Helen Clifford (eds), *Consumers and Luxury: Consumer culture in Europe 1650–1850* (Manchester, 1999), p.192. LeRoy's surviving account books from 1812 and 1821 show that he had 56 British clients, 33 of whom had titles.

13. See Françoise Tétart-Vittu and Piedade da Silveira, *Au Paradis des Dames* (Paris, 1992), pp.16, 18–19, 35, cited in Pamela A. Parmal and Didier Grumbach, *Fashion Show Paris Style* (Hamburg, 2006), pp.53–7

14. Edwina Ehrman, 'Frith and Fashion' in Mark Bills and Vivien Knight (eds), *William Powell Frith: Painting the Victorian Age* (New Haven and London, 2006), p.117

15. Rudolph Ackermann, 'Bridal Dress', *Repository of Arts, Literature, Commerce, Manufactures, Fashion and Politics* (June 1816)

16. Simon Jervis, 'Rudolph Ackermann' in Celina Fox (ed.), *London: World City 1800–40* (New Haven and London, 1992), p.105

17. 'Marriage of the Earl of Wilton', *Bristol Mercury* (8 December 1821)

18. *Observateur des Modes*, no. 26 (1820), where the bride is described as wearing a 'voile de dentelle, bouquet et chapeau de fleurs d'orange' (a lace veil, nosegay and headdress of orange-blossom); and *La Petite Modiste* (1820)

19. Alice Fairfax Lucy (ed.), *Mistress of Charlecote: The Memoirs of Mary Elizabeth Lucy 1803–89* (London, 2002), p.30

20. William Felkin, *A History of the Machine-Wrought Hosiery and Lace Manufactures* (London, 1867), p.409

21. 'London Friday July 19', *Caledonian Mercury* (22 July 1816); 'Nuptial Dresses of Her Royal Highness Princess Charlotte' in *[A Description?] of the Royal Marriage, Consisting of Original Memoirs of Prince Leopold and Princess Charlotte* (London, 1816), p.38, reproduced in Kay Staniland, *In Royal Fashion: The Clothes of Princess Charlotte of Wales and Queen Victoria 1796–1901* (London, 1997), p.184. Princess Charlotte's dress was made by Mrs Triaud.

22. 'Ladies' Dresses', *Observer* (16 February 1840); Mrs Peachey, *The Royal Guide to Wax Flower Modelling* (London, 1851), p.56

23. Peachey, (1851), p.55

A working-class wedding

1. Dr Philip Sykas, Manchester Metropolitan University, personal communication, 20 October 2008

2. H.O. Clark and Rex Wailes, *The Preparation of Woad in England*, paper read at the Chartered Institute of Patent Agents, London, 19 February 1936

CHAPTER THREE

1. The 1870 Married Woman's Property Act did not become law in Scotland until 1877.

2. Jeaffreson (1872), vol. 1, p.135

3. Leonore Davidoff, *The Best Circles: Society Etiquette and The Season* (London, 1973), pp.15–16, 49

4. 'Marriage in High Life', *The Belfast News-Letter* (23 March 1847)

5. 'Panorama of a Fashionable Wedding', *The Illustrated London News* (20 October 1855)

6. 'Marriage in the East, and Marriage in the West', *The Queen* (2 November 1861)

7. 'Middle-Class Marriages', *Pall Mall Gazette* (13 September 1870)

8. 1851 England Census, Class HO107; Piece 14666;

Folio 183; Page 2; GSU roll 87787

9. V&A: T.313:1, 2–2009. Knight's coat cost £3 15s, his trousers £1 8s and his waistcoat £1 4s.

10. 'Wedding Waistcoats', Classified advertisements, *Manchester Guardian* (30 November 1853); 'The Manchester Merchant Tailors Company (Limited)', *Manchester Guardian* (12 January 1865)

11. Pamela Horn, 'Mrs Disraeli and her Servants: 1838–72', *Genealogists' Magazine* (June 2010), vol. 30, no. 2, pp.40, 42

12. Monsarrat (1973), p.113

13. In 1858, following the wedding of Queen Victoria's eldest daughter to Crown Prince Frederick of Prussia, Madame Tussaud's presented a waxwork of the couple with the bride in a facsimile of her wedding dress. For this exhibition, and the display of the Empress Eugénie's wedding clothes, general admission to the waxworks was one shilling. Entry to the special nuptial displays was an extra sixpence.

14. Marguerite Coppens, *La Mariée … Princesse d'un Jour* (Brussels, 2001), pp.35–6

15. Miles Lambert, *Fashion in Photographs 1860–80* (London, 1991), pp.10–11

16. 'Marion's Photographic Wedding Cards', *Daily News* (5 November 1859)

17. Nigel Arch and Joanna Marschner, *Royal Wedding Dresses from the Royal Ceremonial Dress Collection at Kensington Palace* (London, 2003), pp.10–11

18. Fairfax Lucy (2002), p.131

19. This formal ceremony was an important social rite of passage for unmarried girls who had the elite status to attend court. Although presentations took place in the afternoon, regulations laid down by the Lord Chamberlain's Office dictated that women wear evening dress with trains of a specific size, veils and feathers. The next occasion on which a woman was presented at court was as a newlywed wife, when most women wore their wedding gowns modified for evening wear by shortening or removing the sleeves and lowering the décolletage.

20. 'The Marriage of Mdlle. Patti', *Manchester Guardian* (30 July 1868)

21. Jacqueline Hope-Nicholson (ed.), *Life Amongst the Troubridges: Journals of a Young Victorian 1873–84* (London, 1966), p.61

22. 'A Fashionable Quakers' Wedding', *Liverpool Mercury* (24 September 1867) reprinted from the *Bristol Post*. The wedding was satirized as 'Doves in Peacocks' Feathers' in *Punch* (5 October 1867).

23. Richard Seebohm, *Five Generations of Quaker Seebohms: 1790–1990*, edited and updated talk for the Hitchin Historical Society, 24 February 1994, www. prestonherts.co.uk (accessed 25 March 2010)

24. 'Marriage of the Duke of Norfolk to Lady Flora Hastings', *Liverpool Mercury* (22 November 1877)

25. Patricia Wardle, *Victorian Lace* (London, 1986), pp.38–9

26. 'Bridal Economy', *The Graphic* (3 September 1881)

27. 'The Wedding Exhibition', *The Era* (10 December 1881)

28. In 1895 the twenty-eight-year-old widow married an English engineer, Urban Hanlon Broughton. From 1912 they lived in London.

29. Maud Messel went to Sarah Fullerton Monteith Young for her wedding dress in 1898 and as a young married woman. See Lou Taylor, 'The Wardrobe of Mrs Leonard Messel 1895–1920' in Breward et al. (2002), pp.121–2, 126–7. When dressmakers described themselves as court dressmakers, it implied that they understood the etiquette of court dress and had staff with the couture skills to make elaborate, made-to-measure clothes from fine fabrics.

30. 'Hon. Alice Grosvenor (Hon. Mrs Guest)', *The Queen* (15 February 1902)

31. Liberty & Co., *Wedding Gowns* (London, 1907)

32. Helen Reynolds, *Couture or Trade: An Early Pictorial Record of the London College of Fashion* (Chichester, 1997), pp.xi-xvi

33. For a 1912 wedding dress with elbow-length sleeves designed by the London couturier Lucile, see Joanna Hashagen, *Wedding Dresses from the Bowes Museum Collection* (Barnard Castle, 2003), pp.34–5.

34. 'The Trousseau of the Year: What Mr Churchill's Bride Will Wear: Juliet Gown', *Daily Express* (5 September 1908); Mary Soames, *Clementine Churchill* (London, 1979), p.48

35. 'Postscript', *The Penny Illustrated Paper and Illustrated Times* (9 August 1879). 'What is the most fashionable bride's costume? A description of the dress worn by the eldest daughter of Lord Norreys … when she was married to Lord Talbot shall be the answer. The bride's dress was of rich satin Duchesse, made *à la Princesse*, with a very long train, and trimmed with Brussels lace, the gown and train being relieved with small bouquets of orange-blossom; and she wore a large Brussels lace veil.'

Too old for white

1. London Metropolitan Archives, St Andrew's Church, Earlsfield marriages. P95/AND1, Item 017. Signed 'Sams' on the marriage certificate. The 1901 census spells it 'Sames'.

2. V&A: T.309B–1982. Spray of wax orange-blossom, British, 1899

3. 1881 England Census, Class RG11; Piece 1765; Folio 69; Page 4; GSU roll 1341425; 1891 England Census, Class RG12; Piece 34; Folio 37; Page 14A; GSU roll 6095144

CHAPTER FOUR

1. R. Nathan, 'Aida Woolf, Dressmaker', *Costume* (1975), vol. 9, p.53

2. V&A: T.65&A–1973

3. Grace Lovat Fraser, *In the Days of My Youth* (London, 1970), p.2

4. 'Wedding of Princess Patricia to Sir A Ramsay', Pathé Frères, 1919, British Pathé: 2398.07

5. 'Our London Correspondence: The Wedding Crowds', *Manchester Guardian* (28 February 1919)

6. Madeleine Ginsburg, *Wedding Dress 1740–1970* (London, 1981), pp.40–1. The imperial emblems included the rose of England, daffodil of Wales, thistle of Scotland, shamrock of Ireland, lotus of India, wattle of Australia, tree fern of New Zealand and maple of Canada. The Princess Royal's dress is no longer part of the V&A's collection.

7. 'The Film World: Pictures of the Wedding', *The Times* (27 February 1922); 'Wedding Films by Aeroplane', *The Times* (1 March 1922); 'Scramble for Royal Wedding Films', *The Times*, (10 March 1922)

8. Jane Roberts, *Five Gold Rings: A Royal Wedding Souvenir Album From Queen Victoria to Queen Elizabeth II* (London, 2007), pp.84–8

9. 'Bridal Veils for Wedding Belles', *Eve's Film Review*, c.1923, British Pathé: EP 052

10. 'Paris Outvied', *Pathé Gazette*, 1923, British Pathé: 302.30

11. Christina Probert, *Brides in Vogue Since 1910* (London, 1984), p.17. The style was noted in a 1926 issue of *Vogue*.

12. 'London Fashions: Wedding Veils and Gifts', *The Times* (6 November 1929)

13. 'A Parliamentary Wedding', *Daily Mirror* (12 November 1927); 'Miss Aileen Guinness and MP's Daughter Both to Wear Ring Velvet Gowns', *Daily Mirror* (14 November 1927); 'London Marriages', *Daily Mirror* (18 November 1927)

14. Marshall & Snelgrove, *The Wedding of Lucy Fairchild* (London, 1928)

15. 'The Summer Bride and Her Trousseau', British *Vogue* (13 May 1931), p.65

16. Margaret, Duchess of Argyll, *Forget Not* (London, 1976), p.49

17. *Brilliant Society Wedding*, 1933, British Pathé: 697.41

18. The earliest version of the dress was designed by Hartnell in pale pink satin for the 'Bride of Today', one of several costumes displayed during the 'Dream of Fair Women' ball held on 27 February 1928 at Claridge's Hotel, London (Museum of London: 28.44). It inspired a much simplified copy advertised by the Army & Navy Co-operative Society in British *Vogue*, 16 May 1928. Hartnell made a slightly different version for Joan Redhead's marriage to John W. Ropner

on 24 July 1928 (Bowes Museum: 1981.8). Similar floral motifs were used on the wedding dress for Princess Elizabeth (the future Queen Elizabeth II) in 1947.

19. Hubert Llewellyn Smith (ed.), *The New Survey of London Life and Labour* (London, 1930–35), vol. 8, p.311

20. Claire Wilcox and Valerie Mendes, *Modern Fashion in Detail* (London, 1991), pp.18–19

21. *The Sketch* (14 November 1934), p.300

22. 'Moyen-Âge Veils', British *Vogue* (11 November 1936), pp.75–6

23. 'Intentions – Matrimony', British *Vogue* (13 October 1937), p.78

24. 'Leave Permitting', British *Vogue* (June 1941), p.29

25. 'Wedding Dresses For WRNS', *The Times* (11 August 1943)

To wed in red

1. Anna Stone, 'Women in the History of Aviva' (31 March 2010), http://www.aviva.com/about-us/heritage/archivist-blogs/anna-stone/posts/125 (accessed 28 July 2010): 'The gender pay divide is clear in the fixed salary scales of the Commercial Union Liverpool office in 1946, where male and female clerks both started on £120pa aged 18 but from the age of 22 increments for male staff were greater so that by the age of 25 a man should be earning £310 pa while a woman doing the same job would expect to take home £245pa.'

CHAPTER FIVE

1. Ernestine Carter, *Magic Names of Fashion* (London, 1980), pp.92–4

2. Philip Mountbatten was born Prince Philip of Greece. Prior to his engagement to Princess Elizabeth, he renounced his royal title and became a naturalized British subject with the surname of his maternal grandfather, Mountbatten.

3. Charles Creed designed women's wear for Fortnum & Mason during the war and set up his own fashion house in London in 1946.

4. 'Wedding Album', British *Vogue* (May 1952), p.81

5. The Incorporated Society of London Fashion Designers (INCSOC) was incorporated on 6 January 1942 to maintain and develop London as a centre of fashion; to collaborate with fabric and other manufacturing firms to increase Britain's prestige and promote the sale of British fashions at home and overseas; and to support the professionalism and high standards of London's couture industry and to represent their views to the government, trade bodies and the press. Its membership numbered around twelve firms.

6. 'Bride on a Budget', British *Vogue* (May 1951), p.25. The dress was designed by John Tullis. For a 1952 Horrockses wedding dress, see V&A: T.166:1 to 7–1997.

7. Chris Hand, 'Television Ownership in Britain and the Coming of ITV: What do the Statistics Show?',unpublished paper, 2002, http://staffnet.kingston.ac.uk/~ku32101/tvownership.pdf (accessed 30 July 2010). Chris Hand, 'The advent of ITV and television ownership in lower income households: correlation or causation?', unpublished paper, 2002, http://www.rhul.ac.uk/Meida-Arts/staff/ellis (accessed 4 May 2010). By 1964 one television licence had been issued for every 4.19 people.

8. 'Bank Employees' Salary Claim', *The Times* (28 January 1955)

9. 'The Young Outlook: Three for a Wedding', *Harper's Bazaar* (April, 1956), pp.108–9

10. 'The Business of Marriage', *Economist* (7 February 1959), p.176

11. 'We'll all go down the Aisle! ... this new camera will put you at Margaret's elbow', *Daily Mirror* (6 May 1960)

12. 'The Wedding: Sunshine Triumph', *Economist* (14 May 1960)

13. *Woman's Journal* (February 1960), pp.28–9, 58, 104

14. Graham Hughes, *David Watkins, Wendy Ramshaw: A Life's Partnership* (Polegate, 2009), pp.26, 28, 235

15. 'love: is this day the beginning of the end?', *Nova* (June 1965), p.89

16. V&A: T.30:1, 2–2010

17. Angela Carter, 'Notes for a Theory of Sixties Style', *New Society* (1967), cited in Caroline Evans, 'Post-War Poses 1955–75' in Christopher Breward, Edwina Ehrman and Caroline Evans, *The London Look: Fashion from Street to Catwalk* (New Haven and London, 2004), pp.133–4

18. David Sassoon and Sinty Stemp, *The Glamour of Bellville Sassoon* (Woodbridge, 2009), p.44

19. 'We are Happy to Announce', *Queen* (21 January–3 February 1970), p.28

20. Anne Price, 'The Bells are Ringing', *Country Life* (19 April 1973), pp.1113–4

21. 'Your Wedding: A Licence to Spend Money', *Sunday Times Magazine* (11 April 1971), pp.34–7; 'Naming the Day', *Economist* (26 May, 1973), pp.68–9; 'You Pays Your Money and You Plights Your Troth', *Sunday Times Magazine* (July 1977), pp.16–17. In 1977 there were estimated to be about 150,000 Church of England weddings every year in Britain, representing a quarter of the estimated 600,000 annual weddings. More than half of all weddings involved a religious ceremony of some kind. Previously divorced couples entering into marriage again were not allowed to marry in church.

22. Prudence Glynn, 'Happy ever after and six silver-plated teaspoons', *The Times* (16 September 1976)

23. 'Royal Seal for Young Designers', *The Times* (20 May 1981)

24. Suzy Menkes, 'Wedding Dress was all the Vogue – in June', *The Times* (1 August 1981)

25. Suzy Menkes, 'Romance in Cascades of Silk, *The Times* (30 July 1981)

26. Vicky Woods, 'Marriage à la Mode: Vicky Woods on the Society Wedding', *Tatler* (July–August 1985), p.94

27. Ian & Marcel created couture clothing from 1979. They developed their own method of hand-pleating silk in 1980 and from the mid-1980s started using liquid silicone rubber to decorate garments and sometimes to seal edges.

28. Vera Wang founded her bridal firm specifically to offer an alternative to women bored with the 'traditional' historically inspired wedding dress. Her aim was to create wedding dresses that fused contemporary and bridal fashion.

A civil wedding

1. ONS, 'Marriages: 1915–98, Proportionate age distribution (per 1000 persons marrying) at marriage, c. divorced men'

2. ONS, 'Divorces: 1858–2003, number of couples divorcing, by party petitioning/granted decree'

3. British *Vogue* (November 1970), p.115

4. *Women's Wear Daily* (6 October 1970)

CHAPTER SIX

1. Couture dresses made by David Sassoon were priced between £1500 and £5000. Rosie Martin, 'Here Comes the Bride ... A Vision in White Answering the Couturiers' Prayers', British *Vogue* (April 1992), pp.200–201

2. Kathryn Samuel, 'The train now standing ... ', *Daily Telegraph* (20 January 1994)

3. François Baudot, *Christian Lacroix, 1951–* (New York, 1997), foreword. Lacroix opened his house in Paris in 1987.

4. Catherine Walker, *Catherine Walker* (New York, 1998), pp.98–9

5. Lowri Turner, 'The omen of the ill-chosen wedding dress', *Evening Standard* (21 May 1993)

6. Jane Turner, 'How TV's *What Not To Wear* presenter Lisa Butcher faced up to tragedy', *Mail Online* (7 December 2007)

7. V&A: T.198–1997

8. 'Wizard designs on a shoe-string', *Daily Telegraph* (11 May 1998)

9. 'And with this ring I thee web', *The Mirror* (29 January 1999); 'Wedded to the Websites', *Daily Express* (27 June 2000)

10. 'The Wedding of the Decade', *OK!* (16 July 1999), p.51

11. For Chanel's spring/summer 1991 couture show, Karl Lagerfeld cast model Linda Evangelista as a 'second-time bride'. She wore a cream suit and carried a four-year-old boy, dressed in white, who acted as her 'son'.

12. Hamish Bowles, 'The Bride Wore Purple', American *Vogue* (March 2006), pp.548, 554

13. 'Why there's so much marriage mania', *Cosmopolitan* (September 2005), pp.241–3

14. 'The special challenge of China', 2006, www.fashioninganethicalindustry.org (accessed 6 December 2009)

15. Pretty Fashions Inc., www.prettyfashions.com/profile_more.html (accessed 6 December 2009). Corina Gertz, personal communication, 6 December 2009

16. Miles Lambert, personal communication, 26 May 2010

17. http://www.statistics.gov.uk/downloads/theme_population/FM2no32/FM2 (accessed 3 August 2010)

18. Catherine Harper, 'Double Dresses for Double Brides' in Peter McNeil, Vicki Karaminas and Catherine Cole (eds), *Fashion in Fiction: Text and Clothing in Literature, Film and Television* (Oxford, 2009), p.109

19. 'Aisle wear a £100 bridal outfit', *Metro* (15 January 2009); 'Elizabeth Emmanuel (sic) launches wedding dress range at BHS', www.bridalwave.tv/.../elizabeth_emman (accessed 9 May 2010)

20. 'Grooms', issued as CD-rom with *Brides* (November–December 2009)

21. Martin (1992), pp.200–201

22. Alex Gorton, 'And the bride wore ... ', *Financial Times* (30–31 May 2009); Elizabeth Day, 'Recession's cold winds ruffle Paris empire of fashion', *Observer Magazine* (6 December 2009). Christian Lacroix went into administration in 2009 and was stripped by the administrators of its haute couture and ready-to-wear lines, leaving only accessories and perfumes.

FURTHER READING

Anne Buck, *Dress in Eighteenth-Century England*
  (London, 1979)
Phillis Cunnington and Catherine Lucas, *Costume for
  Births, Marriages and Deaths* (London, 1972)
Ann Monsarrat, *And the Bride Wore … The Story of the
  White Wedding* (London, 1973)
Christina Probert, *Brides in Vogue Since 1910* (London,
  1984)
Sandy Schreier, *Hollywood Gets Married* (New York,
  2002)

MUSEUM PUBLICATIONS
Marguerite Coppens, *La Mariée … Princesse d'un Jour*
  (Brussels, 2001)
Musée Galliera, *Mariage* (Paris, 1999)
Madeleine Ginsburg, *Wedding Dress 1740–1970*
  (London, 1981)
Joanna Hashagen, *Wedding Dresses from the Bowes
  Museum Collection* (Barnard Castle, 2003)
Anthea Jarvis, *Brides: Wedding Clothes and Customs 1850–
  1900* (Merseyside, 1983)
Paula Bradstreet Richter, ed., *Wedded Bliss: The Marriage
  of Art and Ceremony* (Hanover and London, 2008)
Shelley Tobin, Sarah Pepper and Margaret Willes,
  Marriage à la Mode: Three Centuries of Wedding Dress
  (London, 2003)

BRITISH ROYAL WEDDING DRESS
Nigel Arch and Joanna Marschner, *The Royal Wedding
  Dresses* (London, 1990)
Jane Roberts, *Five Gold Rings: A Royal Wedding Souvenir
  Album From Queen Victoria to Queen Elizabeth II*
  (London, 2007)
Kay Staniland, *In Royal Fashion: The Clothes of Princess
  Charlotte of Wales and Queen Victoria 1796–1901*
  (London, 1997)

ACKNOWLEDGEMENTS

This book has been written in association with an exhibition of the same name and I would like to express my gratitude to all the lenders to the exhibition for their generous support.

Many people have contributed to my research and writing. At the V&A, I would like to express my gratitude to colleagues in the Furniture, Textiles and Fashion, Research and Conservation Departments. Particular thanks are due to Liz Miller and Lesley Miller for their guidance, unstinting support and wise advice, and to Christopher Wilk, Christopher Breward, Claire Wilcox, Jenny Lister, Oriole Cullen and Daniel Milford-Cottam for their helpful comments on the text. Daniel compiled the invaluable list of the Museum's wedding garments which forms an appendix to the book and wrote the spreads on coloured wedding dresses as well as providing support for the project. My thanks too to Clare Browne, Frances Collard, Ann Eatwell, Christine Guth, Sophie Leighton, Keith Lodwick, Noreen Marshall, Tessa Murdoch, Susan North and Sonnet Stanfill.

I am particularly grateful to Louise Squire, Sarah Glenn and Frances Hartog for their skilled conservation of the wedding dresses illustrated in this book and to Keira Miller who has done a magnificent job mounting the dresses with advice from Lara Flecker and help from Sung Im and Rachael Lee. Thank you too to Hannah Brown for making the mounts for accessories, and to Pip Barnard and especially Richard Davis for photography. I am also indebted to colleagues in the Exhibitions Department, especially Alice Sedgwick, Dana Andrew and Elinor Gallant, and to Anjali Bulley and Kaitlyn Whitley in the Publishing Department. Special thanks are due to the interns who helped so enthusiastically with the project, Emily Ardizzone and Carly Eck.

I am also very grateful to Lucy Johnston, formerly curator of nineteenth-century fashion at the V&A, who took an especial interest in the wedding dress collection, making many important acquisitions and enhancing its documentation. She conceived and championed the wedding dress exhibition.

I would like to thank Beatrice Behlen, Sally Brooks and Beverly Cook at the Museum of London, Deirdre Murphy at Kensington Palace, Rosemary Harden and Elaine Uttley at the Fashion Museum, Bath, Miles Lambert at the Gallery of Costume, Manchester and Anita Blythe at Worcestershire County Museum. Many thanks are also due to Valerie Cumming, Corina Gertz, Catherine Harper, Richard James, Stephen Jones, Anna Marie Kirk, Brigitte Stepputis, Philip Sykas and Kerry Taylor.

My thanks to Mark Kilfoyle for his editorial expertise and to Nigel Soper for his elegant design.

INDEX